Science in the Early Years

Science in the Early Years

Building Firm Foundations from Birth to Five

Pat Brunton and Linda Thornton

Los Angeles | London | New Delhi
Singapore | Washington DC

SAGE Publications Ltd
1 Oliver's Yard
55 City Road
London EC1Y 1SP

SAGE Publications Inc.
2455 Teller Road
Thousand Oaks, California 91320

SAGE Publications India Pvt Ltd
B 1/I 1 Mohan Cooperative Industrial Area
Mathura Road
New Delhi 110 044

SAGE Publications Asia-Pacific Pte Ltd
33 Pekin Street #02-01
Far East Square
Singapore 048763

Library of Congress Control Number: 2009926103

British Library Cataloguing in Publication data

A catalogue record for this book is available from the British Library

ISBN 978-1-84860-142-0
ISBN 978-1-84860-143-7 (pbk)

Typeset by C&M Digitals (P) Ltd, Chennai, India
Printed in Great Britain by CPI Antony Rowe, Chippenham
Printed on paper from sustainable resources

Contents

Acknowledgements

The authors are grateful to all the early years practitioners who have shared their experiences of supporting babies and young children as explorers and investigators.

About the authors

Pat Brunton is a research scientist by training, with a postgraduate degree in virology. She has extensive experience of the early years field and provides training for a wide variety of audiences including school governors, teachers, early years and childcare practitioners and children's centre professionals. She is a director of alc associates, an early years training and consultancy company, and the author of a range of publications.

Linda Thornton has over thirty years' experience in education as a teacher, headteacher, adviser and lead officer for early years. She is passionate about developing children's thinking and learning, valuing creative learning environments and encouraging educators to think about the 'why' as well as the 'how' in their approach to teaching. Linda is a director of alc associates and the author of many books and publications for early years professionals.

Pat and Linda provide keynote presentations and workshops at conferences and consultancy and training for local authorities, schools and early years settings across the UK.

www.alcassociates.co.uk
info@alcassociates.co.uk

Introduction

This book looks at the knowledge and processes of science in the context of supporting the learning and development of children from birth to five. It considers the value of nurturing and developing young children's curiosity about the world in which they live and the skills and knowledge which early years practitioners need in order to do this effectively.

> Once children are helped to perceive themselves as authors and inventors, once they are helped to discover the pleasures of enquiry, their motivation and interest explode. (Malaguzzi, 1998: 67)

Why is science important?

Science encompasses both a body of knowledge which explains natural phenomena and the system for acquiring this knowledge through observation and experimentation. Science affects all our lives at every level. It governs the materials used to construct our homes, the processes by which electricity is generated, the way our food is grown and processed, the use we make of medicines and medical technology, and the technology we use for communication and transport. A degree of science literacy is essential for everyone to enable them to make informed decisions about the scientific advances and developments which affect us all.

Why is science important for young children?

> Babies formulate theories, make and test predictions, seek explanations, do experiments and revise what they know in the light of new evidence. (Gopnick et al., 1999: 161)

From a very early age, babies have a strong exploratory urge, engaging with the world using all their senses. As they grow into toddlers they build on their early experiences and become intrigued by finding out what things can do and how things can be changed. All of this early experience leads to preschool children with the attitudes, dispositions and skills to explore and investigate independently. They draw on their growing body of knowledge to volunteer ideas, ask questions, pose challenges, solve problems and make discoveries, gradually building up their understanding of scientific concepts. They will take this experience with them into primary and secondary school to provide the firm foundations on which to build all their future scientific learning.

This is the 'ideal' scenario – one to which every young child is entitled. Nurturing a love of, and enthusiasm for, science will equip children as citizens of an increasingly technological society. Achieving this demands practitioners who are interested in, and enthusiastic about, science and who have the knowledge and skills to provide appropriate experiences for young children based on a firm understanding of how young children learn.

The approaches to young children's learning and development which underpin the philosophies of Steiner-Waldorf schools (Nicol, 2006), Montessori schools (Isaacs, 2006) and the early childhood centres of Reggio Emilia (Thornton and Brunton, 2009) are all based on the importance of children having first-hand experiences of the real world in order to build their knowledge and understanding. Exploring the natural world, handling tools and materials, observing closely, coming up with ideas and reviewing and revisiting these ideas to consolidate learning and build understanding are some of the key features of these different approaches.

When children are able to explore and investigate their immediate environment they develop the attitudes and skills which will make them lifelong learners. Building their understanding of themselves, of their influence on their surroundings and of the effects of their actions will help to shape their identity and sense of self. Experiencing the sense of wellbeing which comes with success and mastery will help them learn how to cope with the challenges of things not working out in quite the way they might have expected. Learning to see 'mistakes' not as failures, but rather as creative opportunities for developing a better understanding, is a valuable skill for life and well worth nurturing.

Starting from the child

In order to be relevant young children's scientific learning must happen within a context they can make sense of. Scientific exploration is best cultivated through experiences that build on children's current interests and preoccupations – the skill of the practitioner is to introduce resources and ideas which will trigger these interests. Colleagues in Reggio

Emilia use the wonderful term 'provocations' to describe the resources, experiences and ideas which they use to challenge children's thinking and stimulate long-term investigations and discoveries (Thornton and Brunton, 2009).

Although early years practitioners have become familiar with the notion of science in relation to experiences for preschool children they may be less confident with 'what science looks like' for babies and toddlers. This challenge is addressed in Chapters 3 to 13 of this book where direct connections are made between science skills, attitudes and processes and the behaviour and actions to look for when observing very young children exploring the world around them. The role of the key person is very important in this context. As the person who knows an individual child best she/he will have an in-depth understanding of that child's interests and preferred learning styles and will be best placed to observe and interpret the scientific learning opportunities which can arise.

Building on the interests of boys

There is much evidence to indicate the need to engage boys effectively in early learning (DCSF, 2007). Resources and equipment that encourage young children to put forward ideas, find out what things can do, solve problems and overcome challenges provide an ideal medium for engaging the interests of boys. The urge that many young boys have to try things out, take things apart and test out ideas can be productively channelled into interesting and exciting scientific exploration and discovery. Boys' interests in movement and playing outdoors can be harnessed into an exploration of materials, forces, the natural world, light, sound and the structure of the Earth. 'Superhero' play can be become the medium for exploring how things work, air, water, friction, gravity, magnetism and light.

The only proviso about this approach is the need to be aware of the danger of reinforcing stereotypical images and giving the message that 'science is for boys' and is not the domain of equally curious and creative girls.

Involving parents

As with all aspects of early learning parents' involvement and the interest of parents in their children's learning are of prime importance in achieving successful outcomes. Encouraging children to be curious about the world, to ask questions and to explore and investigate creates 'challenging children' who are unlikely to change their behaviour when they go home. It is essential that parents and family members understand the aims and objectives of the setting in encouraging children as strong, competent learners so that children do not become confused by mixed messages.

Sharing the enjoyment of exploration with family members through science-based family workshop sessions can often provide the ideal medium for engaging with parents to talk with them about how best to support their child's early learning (Brunton and Thornton, 2006).

The place of science within the UK's curriculum frameworks

All the early years curriculum frameworks in the UK promote the principle of starting from the child, listening to children's ideas and respecting their ideas and opinions. They advocate providing children with a rich range of first-hand experiences by which they can build their own competencies as active, independent learners.

England

In England the Early Years Foundation Stage (EYFS) Guidance (DfES, 2007) places science within the area of learning defined as 'Knowledge and Understanding of the World'. The requirement states that:

> Children must be supported in developing the knowledge, skills and understanding that help them to make sense of the world. Their learning must be supported through offering opportunities for them to use a range of tools safely, to encounter creatures, people, plants and objects in their natural environments and in real-life situations, to undertake practical 'experiments' and to work with a range of materials.

Within 'Knowledge and Understanding of the World' the aspect most directly related to the knowledge base and processes of science is:

- Exploration and Investigation – how children investigate objects and materials and their properties, learn about change and patterns, similarities and differences, and question how and why things work.

However, three overarching commitments within the Learning and Development theme of the EYFS also have a significant bearing on the overall approach to promoting exploration and investigation to be adopted with young children. These are:

- Play and exploration: 'Children's play reflects their wide ranging and varied interests and preoccupations. In their play children learn at their highest level. Play with peers is important to children's development'.

- Active learning: 'Children learn best through physical and mental challenges. Active learning involves other people, objects, ideas and events that involve children for sustained periods'.
- Creativity and critical thinking: 'When children have opportunities to play with ideas in different situations and with a variety of resources, they discover connections and come to new and better understandings and ways of doing things. Adult support in this process enhances their ability to think critically and ask questions'.

Northern Ireland

The Northern Ireland Curricular Guidance for Pre-School Education (CCEA, 1997) comprises seven areas of learning of which two are directly related to science, 'Early Experiences in Science and Technology' and 'Knowledge and Appreciation of the Environment'. The guidance is based on the principle that young children require:

Opportunities to investigate, satisfy their curiosity, explore the environment inside and outside, extend their sense of wonder, experience success and develop a positive attitude towards learning.

Children should be given opportunities to:

- observe and explore;
- use their senses to explore the environment;
- observe and respect living things;
- learn about themselves;
- talk about the weather and the seasons;
- take some responsibility for caring for their own environment.

(CCEA, 1997)

The Foundation Stage Curriculum, which covers the first two years in primary school, emphasizes the need for children to have opportunities for exploration, investigation, problem solving and decision making and states that children should have:

Rich and varied contexts for developing skills such as observing, investigating, organising, recording, interpreting and predicting.

(CCEA, 2006)

Scotland

The new Curriculum for Excellence being developed in Scotland covers the age range 3–18, with children from age 3 to 7/8 years of age grouped together within the Early Level. The importance of active learning is one of the key principles which underpins this new curriculum.

> Early years staff are committed to developing learning in natural and real contexts, familiar to children and appropriate to their interests and stages of development ... young children's learning is most effectively supported through interaction with adults and other children and through play and active exploration of their environment. Curriculum for Excellence promotes the need to view learning and teaching across curriculum subjects and areas as inter-connected and integrated. This is particularly important for young children, who will develop their understanding of, for example, science, language, communication, technology and mathematics from an everyday experience, such as water or sand play, supported by knowledgeable adults. (Learning and Teaching Scotland, 2009)

Within the Curriculum for Excellence the knowledge content of science at the Early Level is defined in a series of statements about what children will experience over the period from age 3 to age 7/8. These are set out under the following headings:

- Planet Earth: sustainability, biodiversity, climate and earth science, astronomy.
- Energy in the environment: energy in food, electricity.
- Forces and motion.
- Life and cells: keeping my body healthy, using my senses.
- Communication: communication systems, sound.
- Materials: properties of materials.
  Available at http://www.ltscotland.org.uk/curriculumforexcellence/outcomes/science/levels.asp)

Early learning and care for children under the age of 3 is governed by the principles of the birth to 3 framework:

> Early learning involves opportunities to play, to interact, to explore, to create and to problem solve. It is supported by environments that are flexible and responsive which can adapt to children's immediate interests and needs.

> (Learning and Teaching Scotland, 2006)

Wales

The Foundation Phase Curriculum in Wales (DCELLS, 2008) covers the age range of 3 to 7 years. It is based on the principle that:

Children learn through first-hand experiential activities with the serious business of 'play' providing the vehicle. Through their play, children practise and consolidate their learning, play with ideas, experiment, take risks, solve problems, and make decisions individually, and in small and large groups. First-hand experiences allow children to develop an understanding of themselves and the world in which they live.

'Knowledge and Understanding of the World' is one of the seven areas of learning within the Foundation Phase. This places an emphasis on encouraging children's curiosity and includes developing their skills in:

- exploring and experimenting;
- thinking about questions and then asking them and listening to the answers;
- listening to others' ideas;
- what they want to find out and how to do it;
- thinking about what might happen if …

The science knowledge base is grouped under four broad headings:

- Places and people.
- Time and people.
- Myself and other living things.
- Myself and non-living things.
  (DCELLS, 2008)

Structure of the book

Science in the Early Years is divided into two parts. Part 1 (Chapters 1 and 2) reviews the skills, attributes and dispositions which young children can acquire through scientific exploration and investigation and at the creating of 'science-rich' environments.

Chapter 1 covers the development of conceptual knowledge, attitudes and skills, the processes of science and the role of the adult in asking productive questions, co-constructing knowledge alongside children and observing and documenting their scientific learning. It also suggests a way of organizing and managing young children's exploration through the 'Spiral of Discovery'.

Chapter 2 examines the organization of space, equipment and resources, at how to capitalize on the wonderful potential of the outdoor environment and the importance of giving children opportunities to experience risk and challenge.

Part 2 (Chapters 3 to 13) then looks in more detail at the knowledge of scientific concepts which practitioners need in order to support young children's scientific learning and development. The information given here has been specially selected in relation to the contexts in which these concepts are likely to be experienced in an early years setting. Examples are then provided to show what these concepts look like when experienced by babies, toddlers and preschool children. The detailed structure of these chapters is set out in the introduction to Part 2.

Part I

Supporting Young Children's Scientific Learning

Chapter Summary

This chapter considers what 'science' is in terms of young children's learning and development. It looks at the development of conceptual knowledge, the fostering of attitudes and dispositions and the development of science skills. The role of the adult in co-constructing knowledge alongside children, being a source of skills and expertise, asking productive questions, modelling skills, attitudes and language and in observing and documenting young children's learning is looked at in detail.

The processes of science are reviewed and the 'Spiral of Discovery' is used to describe an age and stage appropriate process which will enable practitioners to support young children's exploration and investigation in a structured way.

'Science' consists of a body of knowledge and a range of the skills and attitudes which support and extend that knowledge. Davis and Howe (2003: 102) developed this idea further by defining three types of science subject knowledge:

- Conceptual knowledge: an understanding of, and about, science.
- Attitudinal knowledge: attitudes which underpin exploration and investigation.
- Procedural knowledge: the skills of science.

Young children's experience of science should be less concerned with the development of conceptual knowledge, and more focused on those interesting and worthwhile experiences and activities which can enhance their attitudinal and procedural knowledge. Engendering a love of science in young children and awakening the excitement and pleasure of exploration and discovery in them will create the firm foundations on which to build their growing expertise as young scientists.

To be meaningful, children's experiences of science should be based on their interests and preoccupations and should take into account their ages, stages of development and social/cultural backgrounds. Building on children's ideas not only retains the purpose and focus of an exploration, it also leads to some very imaginative and challenging investigations. As children are not encumbered with 'knowing the right answer' they can prove to be the initiators of wonderful ideas, which in turn can be far more interesting to explore than anything most adults would think of.

Developing conceptual knowledge

Many science concepts are complex and require reasoning and mental visualization skills which are beyond the capability of most young children. Indeed, as adults, many of us can find some of these concepts hard to comprehend and certainly very difficult to explain in a straightforward and understandable way. Nevertheless, practitioners need a basic understanding of key scientific concepts if they are to support young children's learning effectively. This will give them the knowledge they need to engage children's curiosity, ask appropriate and challenging questions, manage children's questions confidently and recognize the 'teachable moments' which can lead on to productive and interesting investigations. The background knowledge presented in Chapters 3–13 of this book has been specifically selected to address this challenge.

First-hand interaction with materials, tools and the world around them will give young children a breadth of experience on which to build their understanding of scientific concepts as they get older. Developing a 'correct' concept may take years but it can start with simple activities – dropping a finger of toast from their high chair, rolling a pumpkin down a grassy slope, dropping pebbles into a dish of water, chasing a shadow or swishing a hand across the surface of a water tray to create waves. 'Doing' and 'seeing what happens' is what is important, although this often prompts questions such as, 'I wonder why … ?' and 'What would happen if … ?'

Practitioners will frequently express their concern about how best to deal with children's misconceptions or incorrect science concepts. Robson (2006: 137) suggests that it is better to think of these as alternative frameworks rather than misconceptions, making the argument that this is more akin to what real scientists do when they invent a new hypothesis to make sense of the world. This view is reinforced by Harlen (2001: 19), who states that 'we must begin to look for a right answer that the children can give with confidence, that depends on their own observations: a right answer that originates from their own experiences. This right answer may fall short of "the truth"'. Probing children's thinking by asking, 'Why do you think that?' or 'How do you think we could test that idea?' may well result in further investigations which can help to clarify thinking. Davis and Howe (2003: 110–17) provide a very useful list of common alternative frameworks with suggestions for questions and interventions which may help to clarify understanding.

Educators in Reggio Emilia, whose philosophy is based on nurturing young children as researchers actively seeking to make meaning of the world, address this issue of conceptual understanding in a very similar manner (Rinaldi, in Filippini and Vecchi, 1997: 182). Working in small groups, with an adult as a fully participating member of each group, children are constantly challenged to re-visit, re-view and re-present their ideas through words, drawings and models in order to deepen their understanding (Thornton and Brunton, 2009: 72). During this process the adult may well put forward the 'correct' scientific explanation as one of a number of alternatives being considered. Once children have arrived at an idea or an explanation which satisfies them, their theories are valued and respected regardless of whether or not they are 'scientifically correct' (Piazza, 1999). As with all aspects of the Reggio Approach, it is the quality of the interaction between children and adults as they explore and discuss their theories together which is paramount rather than the final product. As children's experience grows, the original theory will no longer satisfy them and a new one will be formulated.

The words we use to describe scientific concepts can sometimes cause confusion, often because the same word may have a different meaning in everyday life than that which it has in a scientific context. For example, a 'plant' in everyday terminology is usually a fairly small, low growing structure, while in scientific terms it applies to the whole of the plant kingdom – encompassing everything from blue/green algae to trees. Also the term 'animal' in scientific terms includes all vertebrates and invertebrates, not just mammals (see Chapter 3).

Helping children to learn scientific terminology through modelling its correct use will equip them with essential tools for developing their understanding of scientific concepts. For example, it is important to say that sugar has *dissolved* in water, not *disappeared*, and that metals are *attracted* to a magnet, they do not *stick*. This aspect of developing young children's scientific understanding is highlighted in the section 'Developing effective scientific communication' at the end of Chapters 3–13.

When talking about scientific phenomena – puddles drying up in the sunshine or sunflowers turning to face the sun for example – some children will use the phrase 'it happens by magic' to explain what they have seen. This does not contribute to developing an understanding of what is really happening. Carefully phrased comments and questions will help children to look more closely at the phenomena and begin to develop their ideas about what might actually be happening: for example, 'What do you think is happening to the puddle in the shade?', 'Are all the sunflowers facing the same way?', 'Shall we see if they face the same way in the morning and the afternoon?'

A final challenge to address when helping young children to build their understanding of scientific concepts is the tendency towards anthropo-morphism – giving human attributes and emotions to non-human living things and inanimate objects. Worms and snails with mouths and eyes, flowers with faces and talking dogs can potentially create a very confusing world for young children to make sense of scientifically.

Scientific attitudes and dispositions

The attitudes and dispositions which enhance young children's scientific thinking are similar to those which support their overall learning and development. Nurturing desirable dispositions in young children enhances their ability and willingness to apply skills and knowledge. It also fosters their ability to learn how to learn.

Lilian Katz (1993: 16) defines a disposition as 'a pattern of behaviour exhibited frequently … constituting a habit of mind under some conscious and voluntary control … intentional and orientated to broad goals'. Research has shown that children's dispositions are acquired, supported or weakened by interactive experiences with significant adults and peers (Bertram and Pascal, 2002). The younger children are the more important it is to strengthen their dispositions to engage with and closely observe events in their immediate environment and experience (Katz, 2009).

Bertram and Pascal (2002: 248) have identified four key dispositions of effective learners:

- independence – the ability to be self-sufficient, to self-organize and self-manage;
- creativity – using the imagination, being spontaneous and innovative;
- self-motivation – becoming deeply involved in explorations and challenges;
- resilience – the ability to cope with setbacks and to persist with a task until successful.

Scientific attitudes include personal, social and behavioural attitudes such as curiosity, enthusiasm, motivation, cooperation, responsibility, sensitivity, originality, independence of thought and perseverance. Importantly, they also include the reflective attitudes of a respect for evidence, open-mindedness, critical reflection and an ability to accept the provisional nature of knowledge. Significantly, attitudes are 'caught, not taught' (Harlen, 2000: 5) and it is the responsibility of the practitioner to model and display those attitudes which they wish young children to develop.

Encouraging a respect for evidence is an interesting challenge when working with young children. They will have their own theories about why things happen and will tend to look for evidence which reinforces this view of the world and ignore any evidence which contradicts their ideas. Practitioners can help young children to develop a respect for evidence by making sure they always respect it themselves and by using unusual results or observations as a basis for further investigation, rather than as an indication that 'something has gone wrong'. By gently challenging children's conclusions practitioners can draw attention to the need for evidence that is accurate and objective rather than vague and based on opinion.

Science skills

The skills which young children can acquire through investigation and exploration encompass practical, intellectual, communication and social skills. They include:

- practical skills of observation, using all the senses, manual dexterity, fine motor control, hand–eye coordination and construction;
- reasoning and thinking skills such as questioning, speculating and inferring, problem solving, noticing similarities and differences and reflecting;
- communication skills including speaking, listening, discussing, representing, recording and reporting;
- social skills of cooperation, negotiation, leadership, following instructions and behaving in a safe manner.

Handling tools such as buckets, funnels, tubing, magnifiers, tongs, pipettes and magnets and manipulating materials such as sand, water, clay, fabric, wood, plastic and metal will develop young children's fine motor skills in a purposeful way. Achieving this mastery over tools is not only of practical use, it also boosts children's confidence and feelings of self-worth. For example, being able to pour flour back and forth from one container to another without spilling it is a very useful skill for an 18 month old toddler to acquire. Being the 'expert pourer' will also do wonders for that child's self-esteem.

Exploring and investigating using open-ended materials is a valuable way of encouraging young children to utilize their thinking and reasoning skills. As part of the investigative process children will be framing questions, collecting and analysing information, trying out ideas and making evaluations. A baby will do this when he explores what happens when he bangs a metal saucepan with a wooden spoon, a toddler will do this when she 'posts' a ball into the top of a sloping cardboard tube, and a preschool child will do this when he siphons water out of a water tray and onto the ground.

Scientific investigative play provides an ideal medium to support and encourage young children's communication skills. Creating a positive emotional environment in a setting, where children feel confident to put forward ideas and express opinions, will encourage them to talk about what they are interested in and what they have discovered. Exploration is all about finding out – there are no wrong answers so everyone's discoveries are equally valid and important. Young babies will communicate their ideas and discoveries through movement, expression and body language. Being attentive to these forms of communication and tuning into the many different languages of communication which young children use are essential parts of knowing and understanding the interests of the children you work with.

Scientific investigation involves the sharing of ideas – observations and discoveries need to be shared with, and verified by, other people. Exploration and investigation can be a good way to encourage children to cooperate with one another, to work together as a team and begin to take responsibility for their own safety and that of others.

All such skills will need to be practised frequently before they can become fully embedded; children need plenty of opportunities to hone their skills through exploration and investigation in a wide variety of different situations.

Role of the adult

Co-constructors of knowledge

The concept of adults and children co-constructing knowledge together underpins the work of educators in Reggio Emilia (Giudici et al., 2001; Malaguzzi, 1998: 49–97) and this has become the foundation on which good practice in early childhood education in the United Kingdom is based (see the Introduction). It implies a very strong image of children as competent and confident, with their own theories about the world and how it works. In co-constructing knowledge children and adults bring their own ideas, theories, experience and knowledge to any situation and then seek to make meaning of that situation as they explore and investigate together. To do this an adult must acknowledge and value the skills, knowledge and experience of the children they work with as well as being comfortable with not having control over the final outcome of the experience (Jordan, 2009).

Working in this way enables practitioners to follow the ideas which children come up with when exploring an adult-initiated activity (Davis and Howe, 2003) and to build on any opportunities that arise from child-initiated play. In the process practitioners can model the scientific attributes of curiosity, cooperation, a respect for evidence, persistence and resilience.

Nobody can be an expert on everything so it is important not to worry if situations arise, or children pose questions, which you cannot immediately answer. Exploring and investigating alongside the children, trying out ideas and seeing what happens, will help to validate these processes as acceptable and positive ways to acquire knowledge. By co-constructing knowledge together both adults and children will experience the pleasure and satisfaction of discovering something new and significant to them. These are the learning moments that stay with us forever.

Source of expertise, skills and knowledge

To act as a co-constructor of knowledge alongside children, the adult must have their own skills, expertise and knowledge in order to capitalize on those opportunities which arise. Having this understanding enables a practitioner to:

- provide interesting starting points which excite children's curiosity and fire their imaginations: try looking afresh at everyday resources, consider their potential and find the 'extraordinary in the ordinary' (see Chapter 2);
- see the potential in child-initiated play situations and know how to build on them productively;
- carry out realistic risk assessments, know what does and does not constitute a hazard and recognize how to provide children with risk and challenge without exposing them to danger;
- understand the learning they are seeing in different situations and know how to build on this to support individual children's learning and development;
- probe children's thinking with challenging questions which will encourage them to reflect on and review their ideas.

Encouraging children to ask questions

With very young children it is important to remember that questions can be non-verbal as well as verbal. Young babies will be asking questions and expressing curiosity through their facial expression, gesture, stance and posture, through the length of time they spend absorbed in an exploration or by how often they want to repeat the same experience. The attentive practitioner will be alert to these signs of interest and can then use them to provide appropriate experiences to extend young children's learning.

To encourage children to ask questions it is essential to create an emotional environment in the setting which welcomes and values children's questions. Children must feel comfortable enough to put their ideas forward – knowing that they will be taken seriously and that they won't be laughed at or told they are silly. They are entitled to the opportunity to find things out for themselves, guided by a skilful and knowledgeable adult. If, instead, we fall into the trap of giving children 'the right answer' we take away from them the thrill and excitement of discovery, undermining their capability and potentially destroying their interest altogether.

Asking productive questions

Questions can be used to focus children's attention, help them to notice particular features, similarities or differences, find out what they know, pose problems to explore and investigate and challenge them to give reasons and explanations for their ideas and theories.

Closed questions have a right and wrong answer and can often be answered with a very short response. They do have a purpose, in that they can help children to review and recall information they already have, but they do not usually reveal much about what a child is thinking. Fear of being wrong may dissuade some children from attempting to answer a question, while others may feel it is not worth their while to respond if the answer is very obvious.

Closed questions often begin with:

- 'How many ... ?'
- 'How much ... ?'
- 'What colour ... ?'
- 'Is it ... or ... ?'

Open questions encourage children to express their opinions and share their ideas, explore and investigate and transfer knowledge gained in one context to address problems and challenges in another.

These could begin with:

- 'How could we ... ?'
- 'What do you think would happen if ... ?'
- 'What do you think this might be for?'
- 'Can you think of a way to ... ?'
- 'What else could we try?'

Making these questions person centred, including the pronouns 'you' or 'we' in the phrasing of the question, will encourage all children to put forward their ideas and offer opinions.

Drawing children's attention to features and events by asking, 'Have you noticed ... ?' or 'Did you see/hear/feel ... ?' helps to build their observational skills.

The association between cause and effect can be pointed out with statements such as 'When you do ... , look what happens to ...'.

By encouraging children to share their discoveries with others you will be giving them the opportunity to consolidate their understanding and practise new vocabulary.

Reflective questions can then be used to challenge young children's thinking and help them to refine their ideas:

- 'Why do you think that?'
- 'Can you tell me what you were thinking about when ... ?'

Modelling and appropriate intervention

Modelling is a very effective and powerful tool to use when developing young children's scientific skills, dispositions and attitudes. This could be as simple as sitting alongside a baby and demonstrating the skills of looking through a sheet of coloured acetate, squeezing clay through a garlic press while sitting with a group of toddlers at the clay table or holding a hand lens in the correct position when exploring flowers with a group of preschool children. Modelling an enquiring mind, thinking out loud, commentating on what you and the children are doing, being interested and enthusiastic and welcoming the joy of the unexpected are all infectious attitudes which children will pick up.

Knowing when to intervene in children's exploration and investigation – and when to stand back – is a probably the most challenging role for any adult. The decision about when and how to intervene will be based on the practitioner's understanding of what he or she can see happening, any experience of similar situations in the past and a swift assessment of the potential direction in which the children's learning might go. There is no simple answer to when or how to intervene, as every situation will be different. Experience suggests that, unless safety considerations demand immediate action, the practitioner will gain more from closely observing what is happening, perhaps by taking photographs and noting down the children's demeanour, actions and conversation, rather than joining in and affecting the outcome of the investigation.

Observing and documenting children's scientific learning

Observing and documenting young children's exploration and investigation are key to tracking individual children's learning experiences, making judgements about what they know and planning what experiences to offer next to deepen their thinking and consolidate their understanding. Observation involves the practitioner being aware of, and valuing, how children explore the world with all their senses and express their ideas and findings in many different ways through the use of the body as well as the brain. This is particularly true with very young children.

The tools of observation and documentation include photographs, video, notes on children's actions and reactions, written transcripts of children's conversations, tape recordings, children's drawings and pictures, models and constructions. Encouraging children to take photographs of what is important to them, and listening carefully to the exact words they use when talking about their discoveries, will give you a valuable insight into what lies behind their thinking and reasoning.

Documentation is an active process which needs to be carried out throughout an exploration or investigation and not just compiled at the end. It is used to:

- plan what resources and opportunities a practitioner should offer children next;
- share ideas and experiences with children, prompting them to review and reflect on what they have been doing and what they have learned;
- share information with colleagues to gain multiple insights and interpretations of the learning that is taking place;
- help parents and family members to share in their children's learning.

Giving children time

Scientific learning demands time. Time to explore resources to find out what they do; time to discover what you are interested in and want to find out more about; time to learn skills; and time to revisit and repeat experiences to deepen understanding. As children become involved in their explorations and discoveries, they will also become absorbed in what they are doing and concentrate for long periods. It is important to give children the time they need by keeping as flexible an approach as possible to support long-term investigations. Children need to feel confident that they are not always under pressure to complete their investigations to a deadline imposed by adults or by fixed routines. Where deadlines must be set, children should be involved in agreeing what these will be so they are then aware of what is going to happen next.

The science processes

The science processes are a set of intellectual skills which define how we gather reliable information about the world around us. It also describes the way in which we carry out an investigation and draw conclusions from it (Harlen, 2001). The processes of science are:

Observing:	using all the senses to gather information.
Classifying:	organizing objects, experiences and ideas into groupings which make sense to the individual.
Raising questions:	deciding what one wants to find out.
Hypothesizing:	using information to explain why something might happen or to explain a set of observations.
Predicting:	using a hypothesis to decide what might happen.
Planning and carrying out an investigation:	organizing resources, deciding on what to measure and how to record the information.
Interpreting information:	looking for patterns and associations, deciding what the data show.
Communicating:	sharing information, discussion.

Younger children will not necessarily have the experience or the cognitive skills needed to manage all of these science processes. Johnston (2005) uses the term 'exploration' to describe how young children find out about the world. Exploration involves the first four of the science processes – observing, classifying, raising questions and hypothesizing. As children's thinking and reasoning skills mature they become better able to handle the more complex science processes – predicting, planning, interpreting and communicating – and to build their skills in planning scientific enquiries (Goldsworthy and Feasey, 1997).

Spiral of Discovery

The 'Spiral of Discovery' is a term coined by the authors to describe a process whereby practitioners can support young children's exploration and investigation in a structured way. It mimics the processes of science, but endeavours to present these in a context which practitioners will recognize in relation to young children's learning and development.

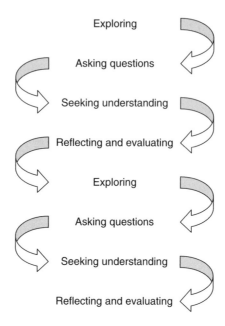

Figure 1.1   The Spiral of Discovery

The Spiral of Discovery is made up of four stages:

- Exploring.
- Asking questions.
- Seeking understanding.
- Reflecting and evaluating.

Exploring

Exploring involves children being playful, using all their senses, display-ing curiosity and making connections as they encounter a new experi-ence, resource or piece of equipment.

When they are in the exploring stage children will have many oppor-tunities to play with their ideas and develop new understandings of experiences, phenomena and events. By providing open-ended resources and experiences practitioners can support and challenge children's thinking, enabling them to make connections in their learning.

Asking questions

Children build on the information they have gained at the exploring stage by putting forward ideas and theories, posing questions, listening to the ideas of others and thinking about what it is they want to find out.

By observing children closely and engaging them in shared conversations and thinking, practitioners will be able to encourage children to ask questions themselves. Children's enquiry and questioning skills can be enhanced by:

- providing the environment and opportunities for children to ask questions;
- placing value on children's answers;
- giving children time to think, to formulate questions and to respond to those questions which are asked;
- practitioners modelling a questioning mind themselves.

Remember, not all children will use words to ask questions. Some may be too young to verbalize their questions or may lack the necessary communication skills.

Seeking understanding

This stage in the spiral involves children in making choices, looking closely, planning what they are going to do, investigating and recording what it is they have discovered.

Children will need the time and opportunity to investigate, to seek understanding and to find solutions to problems. They learn best through physical and mental challenges which often engage them for sustained periods of time. Their investigations may take the form of quiet solitary activities or they might enjoy the excitement of a shared experience with others.

As children investigate they will develop a wide range of active learning skills including:

- reasoning and thinking skills;
- communication skills;
- social skills;
- practical skills.

Reflecting and evaluating

This important last stage in the process gives children the chance to revisit their ideas, to reflect on what they have discovered and to evaluate their findings. This will often lead them into new areas of exploration and investigation, continuing their natural spiral of discovery.

Revisiting ideas and discoveries helps to build children's awareness of their own thinking and reasoning processes. Encouraging children to explain their ideas through the use of reflective questions such as, 'Can you remember what you were thinking when … ?' will help to clarify their understanding. In addition, this will often suggest new and productive ways to extend their experience of scientific concepts.

The Spiral of Discovery with babies

Exploring
A baby sitting alongside a light box placed on the floor picks up a piece of blue acetate sheet and investigates it with her tongue to see what it feels like.

Asking questions
The baby looks through the acetate sheet, demonstrating her interest through her gestures, stance and posture. She drops the acetate so it falls on the illuminated surface of the light box. A second baby seated nearby watches what happens and starts exploring the acetate pieces himself.

Seeking understanding
The baby notices that the blue acetate has fallen on top of a piece of green tissue paper on the light box, creating a very dark colour. She picks up other pieces of blue acetate and drops these on the light box to see what happens.

Reflecting and evaluating
The practitioner observes the baby's interests and offers her a yellow acrylic shape to extend her learning.

The Spiral of Discovery with toddlers

Exploring
A small group of toddlers are playing outside at the water tray next to the sandpit. They are filling and emptying beakers and jugs, splashing the water and pouring some of it onto the ground. One of the children starts to talk about going swimming.

Asking questions
One of the children takes a Lego figure out of her pocket and wonders, 'Can he swim?' The other children watch as she drops him in the water.

Seeking understanding
The other children decide to find out which of the small world people and animals can swim in the water tray. They drop them in and the practitioner draws their attention to what they can see happening. Some of the children try to hold the animals up to stop them sinking. The practitioner takes a photograph of what the children are doing.

Reflecting and evaluating
One of the children notices a plastic dinosaur lying on the bottom of the water tray. 'I am going to make a boat for the dinosaur'. He tries various beakers and jugs to see if he can balance the dinosaur inside them and then goes off to look for something else to use as a boat. Meanwhile two of the toddlers have begun to explore new possibilities about what happens when water is poured onto sand.

The Spiral of Discovery with preschool children

Exploring
A group of children are outside looking for invertebrates in the garden. They have set up a role play scenario involving an outdoor laboratory complete with collecting trays, magnifiers and clipboards. They turn over a stone, discover some woodlice and run off to fetch a magnifier and a collecting tray. When they get back the woodlice have disappeared.

Asking questions
The children have many suggestions about where the woodlice might have gone: 'Into the ground', 'They flew away'. They discuss where they might look for them and search for other likely stones.

Seeking understanding
The children decide to catch some of the woodlice so they can track the journeys they make. They discuss this plan with the practitioner and negotiate who will do what. It is agreed that the practitioner will

(Continued)

(Continued)

find a large piece of paper and will take photographs while the children tip the woodlice on to the paper and use crayons to track the movements of the woodlice. The woodlice move very fast – one child uses his crayon to draw a circle around one woodlouse in an attempt to contain it.

Reflecting and evaluating
The children recapture the woodlice and put them back under their stone. They talk about the way one woodlouse stopped momentarily inside the circle and then moved on. They discuss different ways they could contain the woodlice – string, pencils or wooden blocks – and wonder if they could repeat the same exploration with snails.

Further reading

Davis, D. and Howe, A. (2003) *Teaching Science and Design Technology in the Early Years*. London: David Fulton.

Johnstone, J. (2005) *Early Explorations in Science* (2nd edition). Maidenhead: Open University Press.

Nutbrown, C. and Page, J. (2008) *Working with Babies and Children from Birth to Three*. London: SAGE.

Thornton, L. and Brunton, P. (2009) *Understanding the Reggio Approach* (2nd edition). London: David Fulton.

2 Creating a Science Rich Environment

Chapter Summary

Young children's scientific exploration will flourish in an environment that is appropriately resourced and managed. This chapter looks at the organization of indoor space, the use of a range of common early years resources and the provision of interesting natural, manufactured and reclaimed resources and equipment. It reviews the huge potential for scientific learning which exists in a well structured outdoor environment and discusses the vital role which risk and challenge play in developing young children's scientific reasoning and practical skills.

Creating an environment to support young children's scientific learning involves more than simply setting up a 'nature table' or a 'science display' in one corner of the setting. Instead it encompasses:

- reviewing the organization and use of indoor spaces;
- creating contexts for scientific learning;
- providing open-ended resources which engage children's attention and invite exploration;
- improving the range and quality of the tools and equipment which children can use;
- developing the potential of the outdoors;
- extending the opportunities that exist for children to experience risk and challenge.

Organization and use of indoor space

Organizing the indoor spaces of a setting in order that they promote investigation and exploration involves creating flexible uncluttered spaces which can change and adapt to accommodate children's current interests (Greenman, 1998). If a room is filled with fixed furniture, chairs and tables, there will be little opportunity for children to move around, explore on a larger scale, move materials and resources from one place to another or work together in groups. A cluttered space also makes it difficult to introduce an element of surprise – a huge cardboard box or a tree trunk for example – to stimulate children's curiosity and interest.

Whilst freedom of movement is important, boundaries between spaces – something as simple as a change in floor covering – can help to give children the security they need to become absorbed in their explorations, free from interruption. Resources and equipment are less likely to become scattered around the setting and work in progress can be left to be returned to later (Community Playthings, 2002).

Educators in Reggio Emilia, who pay great attention to the quality of environments for young children, highlight the importance of paying attention to the 'relational forms, light, colour, materials, smell, sound and microclimate' of environments for young children (Ceppi and Zini, 1998). Young children, particularly babies, use all of their senses to explore their world, being curious about what it feels like, what it sounds like and what it smells like. Sensory experiences can be provided by using different textures and materials as floor coverings and on walls and doors. By encouraging children to smell as well as to touch things, we can help to make them more aware of their sense of smell. Try introducing distinctive smells into your setting – flowers, plants, pot pourri, spices, herbs and pine wood. Showing curiosity about what things sound like, and being able to recognize things from the sounds that they make, encourages children – and adults – to be more aware of the environment around them. Add to the sounds around your setting by including wind chimes made of different materials such as bamboo, metal, plastic, wood or shells.

The well organized storage of resources and equipment is an essential feature of an environment for exploration. Open shelves and transparent storage containers enable children to see the resources that are available for them to use. Shelves at a low level can be used for resources which children can access independently and those higher up can store other resources which children can request the use of. Open shelves also encourage tidiness and a lack of clutter. Many types of resources will benefit from being stored in an appropriate box or basket which adds to their interest value: for example, a collection of kitchen tools in a tool box, natural materials in a wooden box or a woven basket, resources for the light box in a clear plastic storage box.

Make sure that the tops of low level storage units and window sills do not become places for 'dumping' clothes, books, water bottles or lost socks. Instead utilize these to display the children's work in progress, models and 3D structures or as an area where mirrors and fabric can be incorporated to draw attention to interesting artefacts. Creating an environment that is ordered, interesting and beautiful to look at will give very positive messages to young children about the importance of their investigations and the value which you place on their discoveries.

Creating the contexts for scientific learning

Many resources commonly used in early years settings have the potential to become starting points for scientific exploration and investigation. These include:

- *Treasure Baskets* for babies from 5–10 months: babies experience a wide range of natural and household objects in order to satisfy their curiosity about, 'What is this object like?' (Hughes, 2006).
- *Heuristic Play* for toddlers from 10–20 months: mobile babies explore how they can make objects interact with their environment to answer the question, 'What can I do with this?'
- *Sand*: a resource to be explored for its texture, mass, composition, ability to pour like a liquid and to take on different properties when it gets wet.
- *Clay*: an open-ended material which can be shaped by applying forces and changed through adding water or heating it.
- *Water*: water can be explored as a solid, a liquid or a gas, it has the power to move things, can effect chemical and physical changes on other materials and has an influence over the survival of all living things.
- *Construction*: construction using natural or reclaimed materials or construction kits can demonstrate the forces of friction and gravity and the properties of materials.
- *Collections*: collections of interesting and unusual objects encourage an exploration of what things do, how things work and the properties and uses of different materials.
- *Small world play*: using small world characters can be an effective way to introduce challenges and pose problems which demand scientific think-ing. 'How can we keep the zebra safe from the lions?'
- *Role play*: playing out the role of a 'Bug detective', a 'Shadow explorer' or a 'Space traveller' can engage children's interest and imagination, involving them for long periods of time in playing out their ideas and solving their own problems.
- *Stories and puppets*: many popular children's stories – *The Very Hungry Caterpillar* is an obvious example – have themes which can act as prompts for scientific exploration. Puppets can be used to help children in their explo-ration, feeding in information, posing challenges and acting as reassuring companions.

The important factor to bear in mind with introducing any of these resources is intentionality. To provide suitable starting points for extending young children's experience of science a practitioner must have clear in his or her mind some broad scientific learning intentions relating to the resources in question. Children are not really learning anything scientific when they are mixing paint unless the activity is set up with the express intention of giving children the experience of solids and liquids, physical and chemical change (see Chapter 6).

Open-ended resources

Light and shadow

Light and shadow are probably the most open-ended resources available to us in our environment but we rarely pay much attention to them. Exploring light, both natural and artificial, can lead to discussions about night and day, the seasons and the solar system and can prompt an interest in electricity and the influence it has on our lives. A beam of sunlight shining in through a window can be tracked as it moves across the room or used to help create a shadow pattern on the wall. Looking closely at shadows encourages the discussion of shape, size and position as well as investigations of cause and effect.

Natural materials

Sand, water and clay are all natural materials which are traditionally found in early years settings, but the range of resources available for children to use can be greatly extended by including a wide range of natural materials to explore and investigate (Community Playthings, 2008). Their irregularity, non-uniformity and variety of colour, shape, size, texture and origin are fascinating and intriguing to children. They invite close investigation and encourage sensory exploration, they are more interesting to look at, touch and smell than plastic and they behave in more unusual and surprising ways. The range of natural materials which would enhance exploration and investigation in an early years setting includes:

- pine cones, twigs, leaves, bark, bamboo;
- seed pods, dried flower heads, large seeds;
- cotton, wool, fur, leather, raffia;
- shells, sand, small beach pebbles, driftwood, cuttlefish bones;
- rocks, stones, clay, polished stones, pieces of ore;
- bones, skulls, fossils.

Each of these categories contains an enormous variety of different shapes, sizes, colours, textures and patterns, leading to a vast array of resources to order, sort, classify, ask questions about and explore.

Open-ended and reclaimed materials

These constitute an enormous range of resources which have the potential to add interest and variety to the plastic toys and equipment found in many early years settings (Curtis and Carter, 2003):

- drainpipes, guttering, tubing, plastic plumbing joints all enhance the exploration of water;
- planks, branches, sheets, rope and string prompt the investigation of structures, forces and gravity;
- fabrics, leather, bubblewrap, rubber sheeting, cardboard and foam pipe insulation encourage investigation of the properties of materials;
- gourds, pumpkins, squashes and pomegranates are visually interesting and all of these roll in different ways;
- glass nuggets, buttons and plastic bottle tops are ideal resources for ordering, sorting and classifying;
- glass nuggets, corks, plastic lids, metal lids and plastic bottles are useful in the exploration of floating and sinking;
- hollow tubes, empty tins, lengths of metal piping and plastic drainpipes can be used to explore sound.

Tools and equipment

Small equipment

Good quality equipment appropriate to the age group of the children is essential to support scientific exploration and investigation. This should include:

- hand lenses, stand magnifiers, sheet magnifiers, binoculars;
- stethoscopes;
- tubing, funnels, beakers, plastic pipettes and syringes;
- large plastic test tubes, clear plastic buckets, collectors' trays;
- small plane, concave and convex mirrors;
- colour paddles and coloured acetate sheets;
- magnets in a variety of sizes and shapes;
- batteries, light bulbs, torches;
- collecting bags, bug catchers, a plastic fish tank;

- child-sized garden tools, watering cans, garden trugs;
- good quality art materials – fine-tipped pencils and pens for children to record and draw their findings.

Equipment should be stored where it can be accessed easily by adults and older children and children should have plenty of opportunities to learn how to use the equipment safely and correctly. Further information on equipment appropriate for use by children under 3, and 3 to 5 years old, is given at the end of each of the Chapters 3–13.

Large mirrors

Mirrors are an endless source of fascination for young children as they invite self-discovery and promote curiosity. Mirrored surfaces positioned at child height on the walls, or on the sides of cupboards and bookcases, help children to see the world from different angles, allowing them to become familiar with the way in which reflected images behave. Mirrors positioned underneath and behind particular resources can be used to focus attention and mirrors on the ground provide a very unusual view of the world. Multiple reflections can prompt a discussion of large numbers, of 'real' and 'unreal', and encourage the use of positional language. High quality acrylic mirrors are safe to use with children of all ages but will scratch if used with abrasive materials such as sand.

Light boxes and overhead projectors

Light boxes invite sensory investigation and encourage children to look closely at pattern, shape and form, to explore transparent, translucent and opaque materials and to investigate colour mixing. Light boxes can be used with a very wide range of open-ended resources – for example, leaves, shells, cones, pebbles, glass nuggets, buttons, large beads, transparent coloured shapes, coloured acetate sheets and colour paddles.

'Old style' overhead projectors, (those which have the bulb in the base unit) are safe for use by young children because they do not get hot. The newer designs of overhead projector are not recommended because the bulb is exposed and becomes very hot very quickly. An overhead projector can be used to explore the effects of light on different materials, make shadow patterns and to create exciting large-scale backdrops on a plain wall.

All electrical equipment should be safety checked annually and all leads must be securely taped down. Light boxes for babies and toddlers are safest if placed on the floor and the overhead projector can also be used at floor level.

Developing the potential of the outdoors

Out of doors children can carry out investigations and explorations on a large scale, experience the forces involved in building and constructing dens and explore the weather and the natural world first-hand (Ouvry, 2000). Growing plants and caring for animals in their natural habitats broadens young children's understanding of themselves and their relationship to other living things. The outdoors is the obvious place for children to become absorbed in natural exploration, developing their creative and critical thinking skills (White, 2008). Exploration out of doors gives children some experience of real-life problem solving, creating the contexts for cooperation, collaboration and teamwork (Filer, 2008). Investigations can often last for extended periods of time, promoting persistence and resilience.

Areas for exploration and investigation outdoors should include:

- a garden area for finding out about living things;
- trees, bushes, plants and a log pile for investigating living things and habitats;
- an open space to move around in to explore the movement of the human body;
- a sandpit for exploring materials and forces;
- the space and resources for building dens to investigate forces and materials;
- buckets, a builder's tray and a source of running water (hosepipe) for investigating the properties of materials, hydraulics, evaporation and change of state;
- wind chimes and large-scale musical instruments made from drain pipes for investigating sound;
- streamers, windmills and rain collectors for investigating the weather;
- an area of soil and rock for exploring the properties of materials and the structure of the Earth.

Experiencing risk and challenge

Enabling young children to experience risk and challenge within a safe and secure environment is an essential part of their physical and emotional development (Lindon, 1999). Without these experiences children will not have the skills they need to recognize and manage danger, for themselves and for others. For children to be able to learn successfully they need to be able to 'venture beyond the known' (Malaguzzi, 1988: 76), to try things they have never done before and find out for themselves – 'What happens when … ?' Tackling challenges, trying things out, coping with failure and enjoying the feelings of accomplishment and success are all integral parts of the exploration process.

A careful risk assessment is essential to ensure that the tools, equipment, resources and experiences provided for young children are safe (ASE, 2001). However, this risk assessment should be done to enable, rather than prevent, children exploring and investigating in interesting and enjoyable situations.

Further reading

Curtis, D. and Carter, M. (2003) *Designs for Living and Learning*. St. Paul, MN: Redleaf.

Ouvry, M. (2000) *Exercising Muscles and Minds*. London: NCB.

Thornton, L. and Brunton, P. (2009a) *Making the Most of Light and Mirrors*. London: Featherstone Education.

Thornton, L. and Brunton, P. (2009b) *Making the Most of Reclaimed and Natural Materials*. London: Featherstone Education.

Part 2 Introduction

The following chapters look at the areas of scientific knowledge which practitioners need to understand in order to support the learning and development of the young children they work with. The subject knowledge presented is not designed to give a complete and comprehensive coverage of the area in question. There are other books, namely those written to supports students working towards Qualified Teacher Status for the primary age range, which do this very effectively (see, for example, Farrow, 1999; Peacock, 1998; Smith, 2004). Instead, the background knowledge here has been selected to cover those contexts which are most likely to be useful for practitioners working with young children. Clearly, it is impossible to predict all the different situations and questions which might arise – that is the joy of scientific exploration – but we have used our knowledge of young children and our experience of early years settings to cover what we feel will be the most common areas of interest and enquiry.

Children's ideas and theories about the world and how it works provide very interesting and productive starting points for exploration and investigation. To exploit these 'moments of enquiry' successfully practitioners must be able to recognize the potential of any situation and know how to capitalize on it. They need to know what questions to ask to extend children's thinking and how to encourage children to formulate questions and challenges of their own. To do this they have to feel confident in their own understanding of a broad range of scientific phenomena. From this knowledge base they will be able to provide resources and plan experiences for children that are appropriate to their interests, experience and stage of development.

The body of knowledge that constitutes science is covered in 11 interrelated chapters. These look at:

- living things, including the classification of plants and animals, habitats and sustainability, the structure of the human body and healthy living;
- the properties and classification of materials, forces including gravity, friction and elasticity, the properties of air and water;

- magnetism and how magnets behave, electricity and simple circuits, sound, light, shadow, colour and reflection;
- the solar system, including the structure of the Earth, weather patterns and rock structure.

Each chapter is presented in the same format. The essential scientific background knowledge is followed by examples of a range of experiences and investigations appropriate for:

- babies under 1 year old;
- toddlers;
- 3 to 5 year old children.

The science process skills (see Chapter 2) which each of the activities promotes are identified in **bold** at the beginning of each section.

At the end of each activity the 'Observe' section draws attention to the scientific skills, attitudes and dispositions which the activity promotes. These are also highlighted in **bold**. This provides you with some important pointers for observational assessment, indicating what to look for to make the most of the experiences the children are engaged in. Careful observation of how individual children behave, and what they do and say, provides important information from which to plan the next stages in their scientific learning.

Included throughout the text are a number of brief '*snapshots*' which describe children of different ages engaged in exploration and discovery. Each one is accompanied by a summary of the scientific knowledge that the children are acquiring through their investigations. These will help you to make the link between the theoretical knowledge base of science and the practical first-hand experiences which interest and engage young children.

Each chapter includes suggestions for developing young children's communication skills by using the correct vocabulary and terminology when talking about scientific phenomena. Language development is essential for effective learning in science as in all other aspects of life. As children master 'the language of science' they will be able to talk with increasing clarity about what they are seeing or discovering, and can thereby clarify and extend their thoughts and ideas.

For each area of knowledge there is a selection of open-ended questions and challenges which would make interesting starting points for further investigations. Remember that there will be many others which will arise as a result of the ideas and discoveries made by the children.

In order to explore and investigate successfully children need to have access to the correct tools and resources. Each chapter concludes with some information on suitable equipment and resources for use with children under 3 years old, and 3 to 5 years old.

3 Living Things

Chapter Summary

This chapter introduces the diversity of the living world by looking at the classification of living things and the characteristics which different species demonstrate. It looks at the structure of plants and the process of photosynthesis, examines the seven life processes which are common to all animals and plants and describes the life cycles of flowering plants, frogs and butterflies. This creates the context for helping young children to look more closely at the features of common plants and animals and how these can be used to group similar things together.

Background information

The classification of living things

To help us make sense of the vast diversity of life on Earth, scientists have developed a classification system to bring together living things which share the same characteristics. This classification system is based on similarities and differences and involves repeatedly asking two questions: 'How are these things the same?' and 'How do they differ from one another?'

Through this process larger groupings of organisms are broken down into smaller and smaller groups to the stage where an individual organism, plant or animal can be identified. The two large groupings of living things which we are most aware of are the animal kingdom and the plant kingdom. In addition, there are three other kingdoms which have an effect on our lives. These are bacteria, fungi and protoctista.

- Bacteria are the smallest cellular forms of life. They reproduce very rapidly but this process can often be interrupted by antibiotics which kill bacteria off. Bacteria are responsible for the spoilage of food, the decomposition of waste and sewage and for causing human diseases such as tuberculosis, typhoid and cholera.
- Fungi live in the soil and in decaying matter and are mostly invisible to the naked eye. They exist as long strands of cells which penetrate decaying plant and animal matter and help to break it down. The toadstools and mushrooms which many of us are familiar with represent the large fruiting bodies of these fungi. Diseases such as plant blight and ringworm are caused by fungi.
- Protoctista are single-celled organisms which live in water. This is a very broad grouping which tends to contain many species that don't fit comfortably into any of the other groupings. Protoctista containing chlorophyll behave as plants and make up the phytoplankton component of the world's oceans. Through the process of photosynthesis they are responsible for generating most of the Earth's supply of oxygen. Animal-like protoctista can be found in marine plankton and also as the protozoan parasites which cause diseases such as malaria.

Viruses are not classified as living things as they do not contain the complex biochemical systems needed to reproduce themselves. Instead they take over the biochemistry of the plant or animal cells which they invade and use this to produce more copies of themselves, killing the cell in the process. Viruses are responsible for human diseases such as influenza, measles, chickenpox and hepatitis.

The animal kingdom

The animal kingdom is divided into two large groupings:

- invertebrates: animals without an internal skeleton;
- vertebrates: animals with an internal skeleton.

Invertebrates

The invertebrate group includes all the creatures sometimes referred to as 'mini beasts'. This is a non-scientific term used to describe a wide range of commonly found small invertebrates. Members of the invertebrate group are distinguished from one another by the features which they have in common. Some common examples of each of the invertebrate groupings are:

Porifera:	sponges
Cnidaria:	jellyfish, sea anemones, corals
Platyhelminthia:	flatworms, flukes, tapeworms

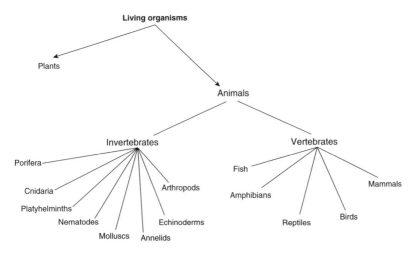

Figure 3.1 The classification of animals

Nematodes:	roundworms, nematodes
Molluscs:	slugs, snails, mussels, octopus, squid
Annelids:	earthworms, leeches
Echinoderms:	sea urchins, sea stars, starfish, sea cucumbers
Arthropods:	arachnids (spiders), crustaceans (crabs, lobsters, shrimp), insects, millipedes, centipedes

Vertebrates

The vertebrate group is divided into five distinct groupings: fish, amphibians, reptiles, birds and mammals. Individual animals in each of these groups have particular features in common which help to distinguish them from members of other groups.

- *Fish*
  Fish can either have a bony skeleton and be covered in scales (such as trout or salmon) or have a skeleton made of hard rubbery cartilage and be covered by a rough layer of skin (such as sharks and rays). All fish are cold blooded, which means that the temperature of their blood is similar to the temperature of the water they are swimming around in. Fish breathe by extracting oxygen dissolved in water using their gills. Fish lay large numbers of eggs in water and generally the parents play no part in rearing the young after they hatch out.
- *Amphibians*
  Amphibians such as frogs and newts spend part of their lives in water and part on land. They are cold blooded and have a moist skin. Amphibians lay large numbers of eggs in water and the parents then abandon the eggs to fend for themselves. When they are very young amphibians breathe by

using gills in the same way as fish do, but as they mature they develop lungs and can breathe air.

- *Reptiles*
  Reptiles such as snakes, slowworms, turtles and lizards live on land and breathe using lungs. They are covered by a dry scaly skin and are cold blooded. Reptiles reproduce on land and lay eggs which are protected by a tough leathery shell. When these eggs hatch out the young animals must fend for themselves.
- *Birds*
  Birds such as, eagles, ducks and robins, are covered in feathers and many species, but not all, can fly. Birds are warm blooded, which means their body temperature is kept at a constant level regardless of the temperature of the surrounding air. Birds lay eggs covered in a hard shell. These eggs are looked after and kept warm by the parent birds and when the young hatch out they are fed by the parents until they are mature enough to look after themselves.
- *Mammals*
  Mammals including dogs, cows, whales and humans are warm blooded, breathe air and are covered in skin or hair. Eggs are fertilized inside the reproductive tract of the female and they give birth to live young. Mammals feed their young on milk produced by the mammary glands and look after their young for a long period of time while they grow to maturity.

Plant kingdom

Plants provide us with food, building materials, raw materials used in manufacturing processes, fuel and life-saving drugs, as well bringing colour, scent and beauty into our lives. Plants also play an essential role in maintaining the environmental sustainability of the Earth.

The plant kingdom is divided into five distinct groups: algae, lichens, mosses and liverworts, ferns and horsetails, and spermatophytes or seed-bearing plants. Seed-bearing plants are divided into two big groups: conifers and flowering plants and trees. Flowering plants and trees can then be subdivided again depending on the structure of the seeds they produce. Monocotyledons (such as maize, wheat and grasses) have one-part seeds and dicotyledons (such as sunflowers, peas and beans) have two-part seeds (see Figure 3.2).

The structure of flowering plants

Within the plant kingdom, flowering plants form the largest grouping which we are familiar with. Flowering plants come in a huge variety of sizes and shapes, possess various coloured and shaped flowers and have leaves which differ in their shape, arrangement, texture and colour. However, all flowering plants have the same basic structure – roots, stem, leaves and flowers.

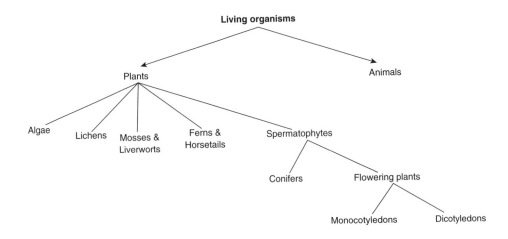

Figure 3.2 The classification of plants

- *Roots*
  The roots are the part of the plant which is normally underground. Their function is to anchor the plant firmly so it doesn't fall over as it grows, and to draw up water from the soil. The cells of the plant need this water to keep them swollen up and pressing against each other. This is what gives a plant much of its shape, and explains why a plant droops and wilts when it isn't watered.

  If you look carefully at the roots of some plants you will be able to see the tiny root hairs which absorb water found around soil particles. This water is drawn up a system of tubes inside the stem of the plant to the leaves through a process called transpiration. On the surface of the leaf there are tiny holes called stomata. Here small amounts of water evaporate and turn into water vapour (see Chapter 7). This creates a tiny negative pressure which draws in more water from the cells of the plant and up from the roots.

- *Stem and leaves*
  Some stems are thick and strong and upright, others are thin and flexible and can bend easily so the plant can climb over and around things. The leaves may be small or large, but are always arranged on the plant to give maximum exposure to the light. In springtime, try standing underneath a sycamore or horsechestnut tree and looking upwards – notice how the branches and leaves are arranged to face the light.

- *Flowers*
  Some plants have large, colourful, scented flowers and others have tiny flowers that are almost insignificant. The flower is the reproductive organ of the plant and contains both male and female parts. The male parts are

called the stamens and produce pollen. The female part is called the carpel and contain the ovules which, when fertilized, turn into seeds.

During fertilization pollen from the male parts of the plant is transferred to another flower by the wind or by insects. Plants which rely on insects for fertilization have brightly coloured, scented flowers and produce a sugary substance called nectar to encourage insects to visit them.

Once a flower is fertilized the petals die off, the seeds start to grow and the seed case swells and sometimes hardens to protect the seeds. When the seeds are ripe they are ready to be distributed in different ways to start growing into new plants again. Seeds such as dandelions travel on the wind, while Busy Lizzies have exploding seed pods which shoot their seeds out and blackberry seeds have a sweet juicy covering which birds eat and will then deposit the seeds in their droppings.

Photosynthesis

Plants are the only living things which can make their own food by using energy from the sun. The green parts of the plant – the stem and the leaves – get their colour from the chemical chlorophyll which is found inside plant cells. Using energy from sunlight, chlorophyll converts water from the soil and carbon dioxide from the air into sugar. This is the process known as photosynthesis.

$$6CO_2 + 6H_2O \xrightarrow{\text{energy from sunlight}} C_6H_{12}O_6 + 6O_2$$

carbon dioxide   water   glucose   oxygen

Oxygen is formed as a by-product of the production of glucose in the photosynthesis process. This is released into the atmosphere to provide the oxygen in the air we breathe.

Children can often become confused when we talk about 'feeding' plants to help them grow. Plant food or fertilizer contains minerals and nutrients which we use to help plants to grow stronger or larger, but these are not essential for plant growth.

Life processes

Although there is such a huge diversity of living things in the world all plants and animals share seven essential life processes. These are nutrition, respiration, excretion, movement, growth, reproduction and use of the senses.

- *Nutrition*

  Animals gain their nutrition from eating plants or other animals. Carnivores eat other animals, herbivores eat plants and omnivores eat both animals and plants.

  In contrast, plants use the process of photosynthesis to make their own food by using energy from sunlight to convert carbon dioxide and water into sugars and carbohydrate.

- *Respiration*

  In animals, respiration is the name given to the process whereby the energy stored in food is released to support all of the other life processes. The process of respiration involves taking in oxygen from the air, carrying this oxygen around the body in the blood, and releasing energy from food through a chemical reaction in the cells of the body.

  During respiration in plants a chemical reaction breaks down food molecules stored in the cells of the plant to release energy.

- *Excretion*

  All living things produce waste materials which they have to dispose of. Waste materials produced by animals include urine and faeces as well as carbon dioxide. Carbon dioxide is a waste product of respiration and passes out of the body when an animal breathes out.

  The process of respiration in plants produces waste gases which pass out of small pores on the surface of the plant. Deciduous plants also lose waste material every year when their leaves fall.

- *Movement*

  Animals move in a wide variety of ways depending on the structure of their bodies. Animals need to move in order to obtain their food.

  Plants cannot move from place to place because they are fixed in one position in the soil by their roots. Instead, their leaves and flowers move in response to external stimuli such as light and gravity.

- *Growth*

  The majority of animals grow until maturity, by which time they will have reached their optimum size. Any further growth is then restricted to repairing damaged tissue.

  In contrast, plants usually continue to get bigger throughout their lives.

- *Reproduction*

  Eventually all living things die, but before they do this they produce offspring to ensure the survival of the species. Mammals, the group to which we humans belong, normally have only small numbers of young and invest a great deal of effort into rearing them. Other animals such as fish and frogs produce very large numbers of young which are then left to 'fend for themselves'.

  Plants reproduce by producing large numbers of seeds which are spread by a variety of means.

- *Senses*

  Animals make use of their senses – sight, hearing, smell, taste and touch – to avoid danger and to find food. Different senses are important to different animals – eagles will rely heavily on their sense of sight, while moles use their sense of smell and bats navigate using high-pitched sounds.

  All plants are sensitive to light and gravity while some, including the Venus Fly Trap and the Mimosa, also respond to touch.

Life cycles

All plants and animals go through a cycle of life from birth to maturity to death. During this process plants and some animals undergo some interesting changes in shape and structure.

Plants

Most plants begin life as seeds. Optimal conditions for the germination of a seed and the subsequent growth of a plant include:

- soil that has been warmed by the sun;
- sufficient daylight as the days get longer;
- an adequate supply of water;
- soil which contains an adequate supply of mineral nutrients;
- a supply of carbon dioxide in the surrounding air;
- space in which to grow;
- protection from being blown away, squashed or washed away;
- the absence of animals which would eat the plant.

When seeds such as beans germinate they produce a root which grows downwards into the soil to anchor the plant and to access a supply of water. The shoot then starts to grow upwards. The energy for this initial growth spurt comes from the carbohydrate stored in the cells of the seed. When the shoot reaches the surface it turns green through the production of chlorophyll and begins to produce food by photosynthesis. When the plant is fully grown and mature it produces flowers which when pollinated will mature into seeds to form the next generation of that plant species.

Amphibians

Amphibians such as frogs and toads undergo a very striking change in shape as they mature into adults. In the spring mature female frogs, which normally inhabit damp shady areas, return to ponds in order to breed. They lay their eggs – frogspawn – in the water where it is fertilized by male frogs. The fertilized eggs mature into tadpoles which hatch out and feed on algae in the pond. Over a period of weeks the tadpoles increase in size and begin to develop legs. Gradually their tails shrink, their gills disappear and they become small froglets, able to breathe air. As they mature they grow in size and change from being herbivores to being carnivores as they feed on flies, beetles and earthworms.

Butterflies and moths

Butterflies and moths go through a process known as metamorphosis as they mature from eggs into adults. Once a female butterfly has mated with a male butterfly she lays her eggs on the underside of the leaf of the type of plant which will be a good source of food for the babies. When the eggs hatch small caterpillars emerge and immediately begin feeding. As the caterpillars feed they grow in size, often very quickly. When a caterpillar has reached its full size it sheds its skin and turns into a pupa or chrysalis. In the wild, butterflies may hibernate in this state ready to emerge again when the weather warms up the following year. Inside the chrysalis the cells of the caterpillar are reorganized and reconstituted into a new structure and shape. At the end of the hibernation period the chrysalis breaks open and a butterfly emerges. As soon as the wings have hardened the butterfly will fly away, begin feeding and start to look for a mate.

Contexts for learning about living things

Babies

Songs and rhymes can help to **consolidate young children's understanding** of the first-hand experiences they have of living things in the real world. They provide starting points for introducing very young children to the complexity of the natural world, helping them to begin **sorting and classifying living things** according to where they live and how they behave.

>> **Action rhymes**

Play a range of action games which feature different types of animals. These could include:

Two little dicky birds
Two little dicky birds,
Sitting on a wall,
(Hold up one finger of each hand)

One called Peter and one called Paul.
Fly away Peter,
(Put one hand behind your back)
Fly away Paul.
(Put the other hand behind your back)
Come back Peter,
(Bring your first hand from behind your back)
Come back Paul.
(Bring your second hand from behind your back).

Incy wincy spider
Incy, wincy spider
(Hold the baby's arm gently in your hand)
Climbed the waterspout.
(Walk your fingers up his arm)
Down came the rain and washed the spider out.
(Run your fingers down his arm again)
Out came the sun and dried up all the rain,
(Make the shape of the sun with your hands)
So incy wincy spider,
Went up the spout again.
(Start walking your fingers up his arm again)

Five little speckled frogs
(Set up five frog toys on a cushion)
Five little speckled frogs
Sat on a great big log
Eating the most delicious bugs
Yum, yum.
(Rub your tummy)
One jumped into the pool,
(Jump one of the frogs off the cushion)
Where it was nice and cool.
Now there are four speckled frogs.
(Repeat until no frogs are left on the cushion)

Wiggly worm
(Make wiggling motions with your fingers, or your whole body!)
There's a worm at the bottom of my garden
And his name is Wiggly Woo.

There's a worm at the bottom of my garden
And all that he can do −
Is wiggle all day and wiggle all night ...
That must be a very funny sight.
There's a worm at the bottom of my garden
And his name is Wiggly, wig wig Wiggly
Wig wig Wiggly Wooo-ooo!

Five little ducks
(Set up five ducks on a cushion and remove one with each verse of the rhyme: bring
them all back at the end)
Five little ducks went out one day
Over the hills and far away.
Mummy duck called quack, quack, quack,
But only four little ducks came back.

(Repeat, removing one duck each time)

No little ducks went out one day
Over the hills and far away.
Mummy duck called quack quack, quack,
And five little ducks came wandering back.

Observe:

- **How the babies move** in response to the rhymes and actions.
- How they mimic what you are doing.
- The way they **begin to anticipate** what is going to happen next.
- Any **associations they make** between the rhymes and their experience of these animals in the real world.

Toddlers

Investigating living things helps young children to see the **association between themselves and the other animals** that live in the world. It is an opportunity for them to **explore with all their senses** and to **make the connection** between their own experiences and the life processes that keep all of us alive.

>> **What does a fish feel like?**

This is a wonderful way to give older toddlers first-hand experience of an animal species which they will be very familiar with from pictures and stories.

Use any type of fish which you can acquire easily and cheaply, but it must be very fresh – mackerel, with their elegant streamlined body shape and beautiful markings, are an excellent example to use here.

Look at the fish with the children. Draw their attention to its shape, and to the position of its eyes, nose and mouth. Look at the fins and talk about what they are used for.

Lift up the gill covers and look at the bright pink gills underneath. Pick up the fish and open its mouth wide.

Can you see how the water passes in through the mouth and out over the gills as the fish swims along?

Encourage the children to touch the fish and see what its body feels like.

Does it feel dry or slippery, warm or cold, hard or soft?
Can you feel any scales?
What does it smell like?

Talk with the children about where the fish lives, how it moves, what it eats and how it breathes.

Make sure the children wash their hands after touching the fish.

Observe:

- How **curious** the children are about the fish.
- How they **investigate** it.
- What sort of **questions they ask**.
- Any **comparisons** they make between the fish and themselves.

>> **Animal movements**

This is a good way to help young children think about the characteristics of different living thing and become more aware of the life processes that are common to all animals.

Use books and pictures to talk with the children about the different animals they know. Look at where different animals live and the types of food that they eat.

Look at a selection of pictures of different animals and talk about how they move.

> Have all the animals got legs? How do you think these animals move?
> Can you find all the animals that run, swim, fly, jump?

Find some suitable music to play some animal movement games.

Encourage the children to try and mimic the movements of the different animals you have been talking about.

> Can you slither like a snake?
> Can you run like a fox?
> How do you think a bird would move?
> Who can be a jumping frog?
> How do you think a spider would move?

Observe:

- The **children's ideas** about how different animals move.
- How they **control their bodies** as they move.
- How they **compare and sort** the animal pictures.
- Any **comparisons** they can make between themselves and the animals in the pictures.

Preschool children

Exploring living things is an opportunity for children to **handle simple tools**, **observe carefully** and **use descriptive language** to comment on shapes, textures, patterns and symmetry. There are opportunities to **compare, sort and classify**, **observe** and **investigate** over an **extended period of time**, **record findings** and **share ideas and information**.

>> **Shapes, textures and patterns**

What you need:

- Hand lenses or a large magnifier.
- Seeds and seed pods the children have collected themselves – conkers, sweet chestnuts, acorns and sycamore seeds.
- Vegetables such as peas and broad beans in their pods.

- Exotic seed pods found in garden centres.
- Fine-tipped colouring pens or coloured drawing pencils.

What to do:

With the children, talk about your collection of seeds and seed pods.

- What shape are the seed pods?
- What do they feel like?
- Which ones are smooth and which ones are spiky or rough?
- Where are the seeds?
- What do they feel like?
- Do they have any patterns on them?

Use the hand lens to look more closely at the seeds and seed pods. Encourage the children to describe their seeds and seed pods and to make drawings of them.

Make a display of the seeds and seed pods, the children's drawings and the words that they used to describe what they were seeing.

Observe:

- How **curious** the children are about the seeds and seed pods.
- The words they use to **describe** what they can see and feel.
- How they **compare and sort** the seeds and pods.
- How they **record their observations**.

  Snapshot

Daniel and Lucas are looking at a collection of dried beans in a bowl – broad beans, runner beans, mung beans, black-eyed beans and aduki beans. 'Are they all beans?' asks Daniel, 'I've never seen some of these before'.

Lucas tips the beans out onto a white plastic tray and picks out the black-eyed beans. 'We have these beans at home. My mummy cooks nice things with them'.

'Let's make some "bean teams"' says Daniel. He and Lucas spend the next 20 minutes sorting the beans into groups, talking to one another as they do so.

'All the red ones go here. They are the best team 'cos there are loads of them' says Daniel.

'Mine's best' says Lucas. 'I've got all the big fat ones. They are going to grow into huge plants like in Jack and the Beanstalk.'

Daniel and Lucas are learning about the variety of living things and sharing their knowledge about how plants grow and what they are used for.

〉〉 Feed the birds

What you need:

- Bird food – seeds, nuts, breadcrumbs.
- Bird feeders – made yourself, or bought in.
- Binoculars.
- Illustrated books about birds.

What to do:

Talk to the children about what they already know about birds.

Look at pictures of common garden birds and draw the children's attention to how they differ from one another in terms of:

- their colour;
- their size;
- the shape of their beaks and wings;
- the shape of their bodies;
- the length of their legs.

Discuss with the children what birds like to eat, and where they might find their food.

Take a look with the children at the different types of bird food you have available – talk about the size, shape, colour and texture of the nuts and seeds. You could also include mealworms – a particular favourite of robins.

Go out into the garden area and decide with the children where you might put your bird feeders. You will want to be able to see the feeders easily from indoors, but they need to be high enough up to be safe from cats.

To make the bird spotting more exciting try creating an indoor bird hide by covering one of the windows at child height with black paper and then cutting peep holes that the children can peer out of.

Choose a certain time each day to check which birds come to the bird feeders to feed.

Help the children to use the binoculars to observe the birds more closely and provide pictures and reference books so they can identify the birds they see.

When you are refilling the bird feeders talk about the different birds the children have seen and which food they like to eat.

Observe:

- How **interested** individual children are in the birds.
- How they **share their ideas and knowledge** about birds and what they eat.
- The words they use to **describe** the birds.
- How the children **cooperate** with one another.
- How children **find the information** they need to identify the birds they see.

Developing effective scientific communication

Modelling the correct use of scientific terminology will enable children to learn how to accurately identify and name the different plant and animal species they encounter. They will have the tools to describe what they see and will be able to share information effectively with others.

large	small	rough	smooth
long	short	round	thin
fat	pattern	stripes	spots
curved	straight	colour	scent
flower	seed	stem	leaf
head	tail	leg	wing
feather	fin	scales	fur

Children will have their own ideas about what it is they want to investigate about living things. These ideas can be used as interesting starting points for further exploration. Other possibilities you might like to suggest include:

- Do birds have three meals a day like we do?
- Do all plants have flowers?
- What do caterpillars like to eat?

- Where do spiders go in winter?
- Do all ladybirds have the same number of spots?

Equipment and resources

Children under 3

Large wooden hand lens
Sheet magnifiers
Large stand magnifier
Large plastic 'discovery' trays
Transparent plastic buckets
Clear plastic beakers and jugs
Small cotton collectors' bags
Small trowels
Woven wicker baskets
Sisal baskets
Collections of wood and leaves
Cut sections of branches and natural building blocks
Good quality plastic worms, beetles, grasshoppers and ants (avoid examples which are not native to the UK)
Good quality plastic frogs and tadpoles
Good quality plastic caterpillars and butterflies
Laminated photographs of plants, invertebrates and vertebrates
Picture books, rhyme and story books involving plants and animals

3 to 5 year olds

Large and small magnifiers
Large stand magnifier
Sheet magnifiers
Small acrylic mirrors
Collectors' trays
Large plastic 'discovery' trays
Bug collectors
Pond nets
Worm farm
Bird feeders
Binoculars
Camera
Simple plant and animal identification guides and posters
Let's Explore Looking Closely Outdoor kit *(Reflections on Learning: www. reflectionsonlearning.co.uk)*

Tolo: Sam the Gardener character puppet

Child-size gardening tools

Collections of leaves and wood in attractive containers

Collections of shells

Collections of seeds and seed pods

Collections of feathers, animal bones and skulls

Small off-cuts of wood

Cut sections of branches and natural building blocks

Good quality plastic worms, beetles, grasshoppers and ants (avoid examples
which are not native to the UK)

Good quality plastic frogs and tadpoles

Good quality plastic caterpillars and butterflies

Laminated photographs of plants, invertebrates and vertebrates

Picture books, rhyme and story books involving plants and animals

Further reading

Brunton, P. and Thornton, L. (2006) *Little Book of Living Things*. Lutterworth: Featherstone
Education.

Garrick, R. (2006) *Minibeasts and More*. London: Early Education.

Young, T. and Elliott, S. (2003) *Just Discover! Connecting young children with the natural
world*. Victoria, Australia: Tertiary.

4　Habitats and Sustainability

Chapter Summary

This chapter looks at what habitats are and at the diversity of plant and animal life found in some common local habitats. It reviews some of the adaptations which plants and animals demonstrate in order to colonize different environments and examines the interdependence of animal and plant life. The influences, including the actions of man, which can destabilize ecosystems are considered and the steps which need to be taken to live a more sustainable lifestyle are suggested. This creates the context for helping young children to recognize the many different types of plants and animals which exist and to discover a little about how they are adapted to the habitats they live in. This will help them gain an understanding of the diversity of the living world and begin to realize the responsibility they have to make sure that these habitats are taken care of and preserved.

Background knowledge

Habitats

The word habitat is used to describe the particular place or environment where different species of animals and plants live. It is the place where they live, eat, reproduce and die. Habitats can be very large – the ocean or the desert for example – or very small – perhaps under a log pile or in a hole in the wall. One habitat may contain many different types of plant and animal living together, each of which will demonstrate the specific adaptations which make it possible for them to survive in that environment.

Different habitats have different features: they may be wet, dry, warm, cold, high up or under the ground, making them particularly suitable for the living organisms which inhabit them. The characteristics of a habitat are determined by where it is on the Earth: in the sea, in the inter-tidal zone, on land, at altitude, in a valley, near to the equator or close to the Poles. Habitats are affected by the climate – the temperature variation, the amount and frequency of the rainfall, the speed and intensity of the wind and seasonal changes in the amount of light throughout the year.

The nature of the underlying rocks also affects the habitat as this determines the type of soil found there (see Chapter 13). Soil is made up of a mixture of small particles of rock, decaying plant material known as humus, water and air. The structure of the soil in any particular place is largely dependent on the type of rock common in the locality but is also affected by how much rain falls in an area. Sandy, gritty soils are formed from the breakdown of sandstone and allow water to pass through them very quickly. Heavy clay soils result from the weathering of shale or mudstone and resist the passage of water. Loam is a mixture of both clay and sand and is relatively free draining and easy to dig.

Examples of local habitats

Looking closely at a local habitat, for example the outdoor area of the setting or the sea shore, can reveal the many different species which live there. These two habitats have been chosen because they are quite different from one another and so are populated by very different plants and animals.

- *Outdoor area of a setting*
  This will probably be planted with a mixture of grass, trees, bushes and plants. Some of these plants will grow well in direct sunlight and some will grow well in the shade. The time at which different plants flower, and how conspicuous these flowers are, will depend on how they are pollinated (see Chapter 3). Grass is unlikely to grow well in areas directly under large trees or bushes because it is unable to receive enough sunlight. Areas under coniferous trees are very likely to be bare because the foliage of these trees is very dense and the soil will also be quite acidic due to the decomposition of pine needles.

  Trees growing in an outdoor area can be identified by looking at the shape and structure of the tree itself, the colour and texture of the bark, at any buds, flowers, fruits or seeds it may have and the complexity of the leaves.

  Broadleaved trees have flattened wide leaves and are usually deciduous so they lose their leaves in winter. The leaves may be either simple or compound. Simple leaves consist of one leaf attached to the leaf stalk. These may be long and thin as in willow, or round in shape as in beech. Compound leaves are made up of a number of leaflets or nodes. Palmate compound leaves have several leaflets arranged at the end of the leaf stalk (as in the horsechestnut) and pinnate compound leaves have several leaflets growing out from the leaf stalk (as found in the ash).

Conifers have needle-like leaves and are usually evergreen so they keep their leaves right through the year. The shape, size and arrangement of these needles help to identify what sort of conifer a tree is.

Any damp shady areas, such as under large stones or pieces of wood, will probably be populated by woodlice. These are arthropods with seven pairs of legs. There may also be centipedes and millipedes which are arthropods with many pairs of legs, beetles which are arthropods with three pairs legs and spiders which are arthropods with four pairs of legs. Looking at how many legs an invertebrate has is a good first step to identifying what it is (see Chapter 3).

Slugs and snails, land-dwelling examples of molluscs, are often found hiding under leaves and stones and are most active at night when there is less chance of their soft bodies becoming dehydrated. Digging in the soil, particularly in areas where there is dead or decaying plant material, will probably reveal earthworms and perhaps the grubs and larvae of beetles. On the leaves and stems of some plants you may find greenfly, whitefly and blackfly which feed on the sap of the plant and are in turn eaten by ladybirds.

The garden is likely to be visited by birds, such as robins, which eat earthworms, grubs and caterpillars, and by seed-eating birds such as finches and blackbirds. Thrushes eat snails, often having a favourite stone which they will hit the shells on in order to break them open.

Squirrels are mammals which feed on bulbs, shoots and the bark of young trees and are easy to spot, particularly in winter when they forage for bird food. Hedgehogs are nocturnal animals which sleep during the day and visit gardens at night to eat earthworms, beetles, caterpillars, slugs and snails. Moles live underground all their lives and can only be detected by the piles of soil which they throw up as they excavate their tunnels. They have inconspicuous eyes and ears and rely on their sense of smell to detect food – earthworms, beetles and insect larvae.

- *Sea shore*
The inter-tidal zone on a rocky beach is a particularly interesting environment because the animals and plants which live there have to adapt to extreme conditions several times over the course of a day, a month and a year. The beach will either be covered or uncovered twice a day as the tide rises and falls. Twice a month spring tides rise very high and fall back a long way due to the force of gravity of the sun and the moon acting in tandem with one another (see Chapter 13). During the course of the year the beach will be exposed to extremes of temperature, drying winds, salt and the action of the waves.

Different species of animals and plants are found at different levels of the beach, depending on how they have adapted to life in and out of the water. Those near the high tide line will only be covered with water for short periods each day, while those halfway down the beach will spend half of their lives under water and half exposed to the air. Animals and plants which colonize the low tide zone of the beach will usually be underwater and will only be exposed to the air for a short period twice a day.

Species such as fish, lobsters, shrimps and starfish live under the water and will be found below the spring low tide level and in rockpools which don't dry out when the tide recedes.

Some marine animals are able to survive regular exposure to the air when the tide goes out by closing themselves off and maintaining a moist environment internally. Sea urchins can do this by retracting their tentacles and taking on the appearance of blobs of jelly on a rock until the tide rises again, their tentacles extend and the animals begin to feed. Mussels, limpets and barnacles will shut their shells and remain closed until the water covers them again. Crabs will shelter under seaweed and stones and lugworms, ragworms and razor shells will burrow into the sand.

Seaweeds are plants adapted to life in water, and to the battering of the waves, by having a tough and flexible structure and being fixed to rocks and stones by a strong holdfast which takes the place of the roots. They are covered in a thick slimy layer which prevents them from drying out at low tide and some have air bladders in the fronds to hold them up in the water, closer to the sunlight.

Birds will frequent the shoreline to find food, moving up and down as the tide ebbs and flows. Some feed on fish, some dig in the sand for marine worms and others scavenge on dead crabs and fish washed up by the tide. Plants which colonize the area above the spring tide level will have adapted to withstand the salt spray in the wind. These will include sea spurge, sea kale and prickly saltwort, all of which can tolerate the high levels of salt both in the air and in the soil.

Adaptation in plants and animals

Animals and plants live in specific locations because they have adapted to survive the particular conditions which exist there. Some obvious examples include the following.

- Spiders can produce silk from a gland on their abdomen which they use to spin a web to trap the food they eat. The shape of the web will vary depending on the species of spider, where it lives and what type of prey it catches.
- Fish are able to live in water because they can extract oxygen from the water as it passes over their gills and they are a streamlined shape so they can move through the water easily.
- Polar bears have very thick coats to enable them to withstand very low temperatures and they hibernate in winter when their food supplies are scarce.

- Desert plants such as cacti can live in very hot dry conditions because they are able to conserve water. The swollen green stem of the plant stores water and carries out photosynthesis, while the leaves have become modified into spines to discourage animals from eating the plant. The stem is also covered in a thick waxy cuticle to further cut down water loss through transpiration (see Chapter 3).
- Trees in dense forests will grow very tall in order to reach the light so that they are able to photosynthesize efficiently.
- Bushes and trees growing in windy places, such as exposed hilltops or along the coast, will be small and stunted to prevent branches being broken by the wind.

This ability to adapt to different environments is the basis of the theory of evolution put forward by Charles Darwin over two hundred years ago. Within a species the process of genetic mutation creates small changes in the characteristics of the individuals of that species. Where these changes give the animal or plant an advantage in any particular habitat the animal or plant is more likely to survive and breed. This then leads to the production of more individuals with the same adapted characteristics – namely, the survival of the fittest.

Food chains

The kinds of animal species found in any habitat will ultimately be determined by the range of plant species that are found there because all animals rely on plants for their food. Some animals, for example caterpillars, rabbits or cows, eat plants directly and can only survive in a habitat which supports the growth of their primary food plant. Other animals, such as centipedes, foxes and lions, eat other animals and are dependent for their survival on being able to access a supply of these animals in their habitat.

All habitats will support complex food chains or food webs which have the producers, plants of every description, at the base and larger carnivores at the top. A typical food chain in a garden might be:

lettuce → caterpillar → blue tit → hawk
green plant → decaying leaf → earthworm → frog → heron

Through this process the carbon in the sugars produced by plant photo-synthesis is converted into the bodies of animals. When these animals die their bodies will decompose through the action of bacteria and fungi and this carbon is then released into the environment, for example as carbon dioxide gas, where it can be used again by plants.

Sustainability

Disrupting the complex relationship which exists between the millions of plant and animal species in the environment can have unexpected and far reaching consequences. Ecosystems exist in a delicate balance dependent on interactions between the environment, the weather, the plant species which grow in any locality and the animals which depend on those plants. These ecosystems can be destabilized by:

- sudden changes in the physical structure of the Earth such as happens when volcanoes erupt or earthquakes happen;
- powerful weather events such as hurricanes and tornadoes;
- the effects of weathering and erosion on the natural landscape;
- burning fossil fuels, thereby releasing carbon dioxide into the atmosphere which prevents heat loss from the Earth and causes the ambient temperature to rise;
- cutting down large tracts of the rain forest thereby lowering the amount of oxygen and water vapour that is released into the atmosphere and reducing the amount of carbon dioxide that is removed from the air;
- polluting the sea, causing the death of phytoplankton which are responsible for releasing large volumes of oxygen into the air through the photosynthesis process;
- the contamination of water sources with chemicals, fertilizers or oil;
- building on large areas of land, cutting down the ability of that land to soak up rainfall, thus leading to flooding;
- destroying wildlife habitats through tree felling, intensive farming, building houses or roads and diverting rivers, thereby upsetting the delicate balance within an ecosystem;
- large-scale mining activities.

Many of these destabilizing effects are caused by the actions of man on the environment and are a direct or indirect consequence of increases in the size and expectations of the human population. This creates an increasing and ultimately unsustainable demand for raw materials such as wood and minerals, for food and for water.

The growing awareness around the world of the importance of addressing sustainability issues has led to moves to:

- decrease the consumption of raw materials by encouraging their re-use and recycling;
- reduce the amount of carbon dioxide released into the atmosphere by cutting back on the burning of fossil fuels and using renewable sources of energy instead: these include hydroelectric power from rivers and wave barrages, wind power from turbines and windmills, solar power from the Sun and biofuels produced by processing plant materials;

- improve building design and insulation to reduce the need to use energy to keep living and working spaces warm or cool;
- conserve and recycle water supplies to prevent unnecessary wastage;
- bio-engineer new species of food crops which are disease resistant, grow rapidly and crop heavily;
- investigate the production of new food crops using micro-organisms.

Contexts for learning about habitats and sustainability

Babies

Encouraging babies to explore the local environment will increase their **awareness and appreciation of the world** around them. It is an ideal way to encourage them to be **curious** and to **explore with all their senses**. They will have opportunities to **distinguish between different sensations** and develop their appreciation of the beauty and complexity of the natural world.

>> **Exploring environments**

When you are outside with the babies help them to explore the different environments around your setting. While sitting on the grass comment on its texture – whether it feels soft or spiky, warm or cold, damp or dry. If the grass has recently been cut, help the babies to investigate what it feels like, what it smells like and what they can do with it.

Take a walk around the outdoor area and draw the babies' attention to how light or dark different spaces are, how warm or cold they feel and what sorts of trees and plants you can find there. Encourage them to feel the bark of the trees and to look for interesting leaves and flowers. Talk about the colour, scent, shape and texture of the leaves and flowers you find.

Observe:

- How individual babies **react to the experience**.
- **How interested** they are in the things they find in the environment around them.
- How they **touch and manipulate the materials** they explore.
- **How long they explore** and investigate for.

>> Exploring leaves

Make a collection of leaves, ideally in the autumn when the leaves are dry and easy to handle. Try to avoid picking up too many damp leaves as this 'leaf litter' is likely to have many small invertebrates living in it.

Place the leaves in a large tray on the floor and encourage the babies to investigate the leaf pile.

Observe:

- How **curious** they are about the leaf pile.
- **What they do** with the leaves.
- Do they pick them up, drop them, wave them around, scrunch them up, lie in them?
- How individual babies pick up and **manipulate** the leaves.
- **How long** they remain interested in their leaf explorations.

Snapshot

Isaac sits quietly on the ground under a sycamore tree and strokes his hands gently over the grass. He picks up a fallen leaf and rubs it along his arm and then on the side of his face before dropping it and watching it fall to the ground. He is using his senses to learn about different types of plants, their structure and how they behave.

Toddlers

Finding out what lives in the outdoor environment encourages toddlers to be **curious** about the world around them. They will begin to develop an **understanding of the variety of life** which exists and can be helped to develop **positive attitudes** towards other living things.

>> Dig, dig, dig

This is an ideal opportunity to help toddlers to develop their physical coordination skills by digging on a large scale out of doors. Provide appropriate size spades and trowels and an area of bare soil which they can dig in. As they do so, talk to them about the colour, weight and texture of the soil.

Is it thick and heavy or light and crumbly?
How easy is it to push a spade in?
You could try tipping some of the soil into a garden sieve and tapping it. What falls through the holes in the sieve? What stays behind?

Look for interesting rocks, stones, snail shells, leaves, seeds, earthworms, beetles or ants.

Try tipping some soil onto a large sheet of white paper. What can you see?

Observe:

- How the toddlers **handle the tools**.
- How **curious** they are about what they find in the soil.
- Any **comments they make** about what they are doing.
- **How often** individual children want to repeat the experience.

>> Woodlouse hunt and a spider safari

Woodlice are usually fairly easy to find in any garden and are relatively resistant to investigation by small hands.

Go on a bug hunt round the garden looking for likely places to find woodlice and spiders. When you find some woodlice watch what they do when exposed to the light. Draw the children's attention to how fast they move and where they go.

Collect a small number of woodlice in a white plastic tray and help the children to look carefully at them. Using a sheet magnifier or a large stand magnifier will help the children to see the woodlice more easily. Talk about their size, shape and how they move.

Return the woodlice to where you found them, talking to the children about the importance of taking care of all living things.

Spiders are most obvious in the mornings in late summer/early autumn when the dew forms on their webs and makes them very easy to see.

With the children look at the shape and structure of the spider's web. Can you see the spider at the edge of the web? Has he caught anything? Listen to what the children have to say about the web. What do they think it is for?

Talk to the children about the importance of not damaging the spider's web.

Observe:

- **How interested** individual children are in looking for creatures in the garden.
- **What the children have to say** about the woodlice and the spiders' webs.
- **How long** they spend **observing** the creatures.

Preschool children

The outdoor environment represents a huge and exciting place in which young children's **skills of observing, questioning, comparing, sorting, trying out ideas and finding out information** can be developed. There are opportunities for **planning investigations** over extended periods of time, **recalling ideas** and **offering explanations of why things happen**.

>> **Establishing a log pile**

What you need:

- An area of the setting which will be suitable for setting up the log pile.
- Some large logs, ideally already starting to rot.
- Branches, twigs and leaves.
- Magnifiers.
- Trays suitable for collecting small invertebrates.
- Pictures of common garden invertebrates.
- Invertebrate identification guides.

What to do:

- Talk to the children about the purpose of the log pile – to provide food, shelter and a breeding ground for a wide range of small invertebrates.
- Discuss with them where it would be best to position the log pile – say, somewhere shady and damp where it is not going to be disturbed.
- Work together to create the log pile, keeping it low so it doesn't present a hazard.

Encourage the children to check the pile regularly to see what they can find. Make sure the children understand the importance of replacing any leaves, wood or bark they have turned over or moved.

You could use the log pile as the starting point for drawing attention to the features of different invertebrates you find.

For example, ask:

Does it have legs?

If the answer is 'no' it could be an earthworm, a slug or a snail.

If the answer is 'yes' then ask

How many legs does it have?

If the answer is 'eight' ask

Is it a spider?

If 'six' ask

Is it an insect?

If the answer is '14' ask

Is it a woodlouse?

If the answer is 'lots' then it could be a millipede or a centipede.

(The classification of living things is described in Chapter 3 and shown in Figures 3.1 and 3.2.)

Observe:

- The **ideas the children put forward** about where to position the log pile and the **reasons behind these ideas**.
- How well they **cooperate** with one another while building the pile.
- Any **predictions** they make about what will happen to the log pile over time.
- How **curious** they are about the creatures they find there.
- How they begin to **sort and classify** the invertebrates they find.
- How they use **sources of information** to help them to identify their finds.
- How they demonstrate their understanding of the **importance of caring for living things**.

 ## Snapshot

A group of 4 year olds became so fascinated with their investigations in the log pile that they set up a role play area out of doors, equipped with magnifiers, binoculars, beakers, collecting trays and clipboards. They explored the log pile and the surrounding garden as 'nature detectives' and recorded what they found using the clipboards.

Through this process they were learning about the classification of living things, habitats and adaptations in plants and animals.

>> Looking at flowers

What you need:

- Magnifying glasses or sheet magnifiers.
- An area outdoors where there is a range of different flowering plants growing.
- Drawing paper and pencils.

What to do:

This activity encourages children to notice flowers in the environment around them and to look carefully at their different shapes and structures.

- Choose an area which contains a variety of different flowers – discuss the importance of handling the plants gently.
- Look at the flowers together and talk about what you can see.
- How many different types of flowers are there?
- What shape is each of the flowers?
- How many petals do each of the different flowers have?
- Are the petals individual (as in a daisy), or are they joined on to one another (as in a daffodil)?
- What colours are the petals?
- What colour is the centre of the flower?

This is a good opportunity to make a simple record or tally sheet of the numbers of the different plants you find.

Help the children to use the magnifiers to look closely at the structure of the different flowers.

Talk about what you can see.

Encourage the children to make drawings of the flowers and to talk about what they look like.

Some of the children may prefer to make representations of the flowers using small pieces of fabric, coloured cellophane and scraps of reclaimed materials.

Observe:

- How carefully the children **observe, using all their senses**.
- How they **describe** what they can see.
- How they **record their observations**.
- How they **manipulate the tools** they use.

Developing effective scientific communication

Helping children to learn the correct terminology to describe the different plants and animals which they discover in the environment will enable them to describe similarities and difference accurately, simplifying the processes of sorting and classifying.

flower	petal	stem	leaf
root	home	food	safe
log	pile	rot	branch
leaves	hide	damp	snail
slug	earthworm	beetle	caterpillar
butterfly	bee	ladybird	ant
woodlouse	spider	legs	shell
wings	web	silk	spin

The children's investigations of the outdoor environment will generate lots of interesting ideas which you will be able to capitalize on to develop their scientific thinking and investigative skills. Other possibilities you might like to explore are:

- Do all snails have the same patterns on their shells?
- What sorts of plants do butterflies like best?
- What do worms like to eat?
- Are all slugs slimy?
- Where do beetles go when it rains?
- Could we track the journeys that the woodlice take?
- Do all plants like to grow in sunny places?
- What happens to the leaves when they fall off the trees in autumn?
- Can plants move?

Equipment and resources

Children under 3

Large wooden hand lens
Sheet magnifiers
Large stand magnifier
Large plastic 'discovery' trays
Transparent plastic buckets
Clear plastic beakers and jugs
Small trowels

Small cotton collectors' bags

Woven wicker baskets

Sisal baskets

Collections of large pebbles and stones

Collections of wood and leaves

Cut sections of branches and natural building blocks

Good quality plastic worms, beetles, grasshoppers and ants (avoid examples which are not native to the UK)

Good quality plastic frogs and tadpoles

Good quality plastic caterpillars and butterflies

Laminated photographs of plants, invertebrates and vertebrates

Picture books, rhyme and story books involving plants and animals

3 to 5 year olds

Large and small magnifiers

Large stand magnifier

Sheet magnifiers

Small acrylic mirrors

Collectors' trays

Large plastic 'discovery' trays

Bug collectors

Pond nets

Worm farm

Bird feeders

Binoculars

Camera

Simple plant and animal identification guides and posters

Tolo: Sam the Gardener character puppet

Child-sized gardening tools

Sieves

Let's Explore Growing Plants kit (*Reflections on Learning: www.reflectionsonlearning. co.uk*)

Let's Explore Looking Closely Outdoor kit (*Reflections on Learning: www. reflectionsonlearning.co.uk*)

Collections of leaves and wood in attractive containers

Collections of shells

Collections of seeds and seed pods

Collections of feathers, animal bones and skulls

Small off-cuts of wood

Cut sections of branches and natural building blocks

Good quality plastic worms, beetles, grasshoppers and ants (avoid examples which are not native to the UK)

Good quality plastic frogs and tadpoles
Good quality plastic caterpillars and butterflies
Laminated photographs of plants, invertebrates and vertebrates
Picture books, rhyme and story books involving plants and animals

Further reading

Brunton, P. and Thornton, L. (2006) *Little Book of Living Things*. Lutterworth: Featherstone Education.

De Boo, M. (2005) *Nature Detectives*. Hatfield: Association for Science Education.

Garrick, R. (2006) *Minibeasts and More*. London: Early Education.

Osband, G. (1990) *Investigating the Sea Shore*. London: National Trust.

Young, T. and Elliott, S. (2003) *Just Discover! Connecting young children with the natural world*. Victoria, Australia: Tertiary.

5 The Structure of the Human Body and Healthy Living

Chapter Summary

This chapter looks at the structure and function of the main organ systems of the human body and how they work together to keep us alive. It reviews how healthy eating, physical exercise and emotional wellbeing contribute to living a healthy lifestyle and the importance to children of having strong positive relationships with their parents and carers. This creates the context for helping young children to learn more about how their bodies work to enable them to gain mastery over themselves and their surroundings. There are opportunities for children to make choices and to feel confident in expressing their feelings and emotions.

Background information

The structure of the human body

The human body is a complex system of organs, structures and control mechanisms which interact with one another to produce a healthy, functioning individual. It consists of:

- a framework comprising the bones of the skeleton, the muscles and the skin;
- the cardiovascular system made up of the heart, lungs, blood and circulatory system;
- the nervous system including the brain, spinal cord and nerves;
- sense organs including the eye, ear, nose and tongue;
- the digestive system including the mouth, oesophagus, stomach, intestines and liver;

- the excretory system made up of the kidneys and the bladder;
- the endocrine system comprising the endocrine glands and hormones;
- a reproductive system including the ovaries, uterus, testicles and penis.

Skeleton, muscles and skin

Humans are vertebrates and have a backbone and an internal skeleton. The skeleton supports the body, provides attachment points for muscles so we can move and protects the internal organs.

Bone is a living tissue made up of protein and minerals, largely calcium and phosphorous. The ends of the bones are covered with a smooth layer of material called cartilage. The design of the joint determines which way the bones can move. Hinge joints as in the elbow or knee allow movement in only one direction: ball and socket joints in the hips and shoulders permit rotational movement.

Muscles work in pairs to facilitate movement: when one muscle in the pair contracts, the other relaxes. Muscles need energy in order to move and this energy comes from the food we eat. Some muscles, in the arm and the leg for example, are under our voluntary control. Other muscles, such as those in the heart and the stomach, work involuntarily and are not under our direct control.

The motor neurones of the nervous system transmit messages from the brain to the muscles to stimulate them to move. Feedback to the brain comes from the sensory nerves which transmit messages about what is happening in every part of the body.

The cardiovascular and excretory systems

The function of the cardiovascular system is to pump oxygenated blood around the body, to carry food molecules to the cells to provide energy and to take away waste products including carbon dioxide.

Blood is made up of red blood cells which help to carry oxygen around the body, white blood cells which help to fight infection and plasma, platelets and a protein called fibrinogen. When we cut ourselves blood flows out from the damaged blood vessels. The protein fibrinogen, when exposed to air, forms a mesh to trap the platelets in the blood. This slows down the flow of blood until the bleeding eventually stops. Disturbing the clot will make the blood start flowing again.

The heart is a pump made of muscle tissue which beats constantly. It is divided into two halves and each half has two chambers with a valve between them. Blood flows into one half of the heart from the large veins in the body and the heart muscle then pumps this blood to the lungs.

In the lungs the blood picks up oxygen from the air we breathe and then flows back to the other half of the heart. The oxygenated blood is then pumped by the heart along the arteries to all parts of the body. The pulse we can feel in our wrist or neck is caused by the pumping action of the heart.

Blood passes round the body in a system of arteries, capillaries and veins. Oxygen passes from the capillaries into the cells of the body and waste products, including carbon dioxide, pass from the cells into the blood vessels. When we exercise the blood flow to the skin increases to bring more blood closer to the surface to cool it down. As a consequence of this we appear hot and flushed. When we are frightened the nervous system redirects the blood flow away from the organs to provide more oxygen and energy for the muscles. This is why we appear pale and wan.

On its journey around the body the blood passes through the kidneys. Here water and waste products are removed and transported to the bladder where they are stored temporarily before they pass out of the body as urine.

The lungs in the chest are protected by the rib cage, the backbone and the sternum or breastbone and separated from the other organs by a smooth sheet of muscle called the diaphragm. This creates a closed chamber in which the lungs can inflate and deflate as we breathe in and out. When we breathe in the chest muscles contract and lift the ribs up and pull the diaphragm downwards. This increases the volume of the chest cavity so the lungs can expand and air is drawn in. When we breathe out the muscles in the chest wall and the diaphragm relax so the diaphragm balloons upwards and the size of the chest cavity decreases. This squeezes air out of the lungs. All these movements involved in breathing happen automatically, although we can control them if we want to.

The nervous system

The nervous system, consisting of the brain and the nerves, controls all of the organ systems of the body. The sensory nerves carry information from the sense organs to the brain and the motor nerves carry messages from the brain to the muscles to make them move.

The brain is made up of millions of nerve cells called neurones which link together in networks. The brain has three main parts – the cerebrum, the cerebellum and the brain stem. The cerebrum is the largest part of the brain and is divided into the right and left hemispheres. The right hemisphere controls the left side of the body and the left hemisphere controls the right side of the body. The cerebrum controls all the higher brain functions – thought, feelings, behaviour and memory. It is where information from the sense organs is processed and where language and speech originate.

The cerebellum is at the back of the head and is much smaller that the cerebrum. It regulates balance and posture. The brain stem controls all the basic functions that keep us alive, including breathing, heartbeat, blood pressure and swallowing.

Brain development begins during pregnancy and there are critical periods when an exposure to harmful chemicals can have devastating consequences for the unborn baby. At birth the brain consists of over 1000 billion neurons, but is not yet mature as the connections between the different neurons have still to be generated.

As a baby responds to the world around him – through sight, hearing, touch, taste and smell – messages are sent along the neurons in the brain. These messages pass from one neuron to another across a bridge known a synapse. The more different stimuli the brain receives, and the more often a stimulus is repeated, the greater the number of synapses that form.

During the first three years of life the brain creates more synapses than it needs. Thereafter, those synapses that are rarely used die off and are eliminated. The experiences a young child has in the first years of life are vitally important for his or her overall learning and development, but learning does not stop at age three, it goes on throughout life.

Sense organs

Most of the sense organs are on the head where they are close to the brain so messages can be responded to quickly.

We use our eyes and our sense of sight to tell us most about what is happening around us. Light from a light source, or reflected from the surface of an object, travels outwards in straight lines (see Chapter 12). When this light passes through the lens at the front of the eyeball the rays of light are bent to focus an image on the retina at the back of the eye. Electrical impulses then carry messages from each eye along the optic nerve to the brain. This information is processed in the brain to produce three-dimensional coloured images – this is what we 'see'.

Our sense of hearing is our second most important sense. Having an ear on either side of our head helps us to work out the direction a sound is coming from. Sound vibrations in the air travel outwards in waves from the object making the sound (see Chapter 11). Some of these waves will reach the ears and travel along the ear canal to the eardrum causing it to vibrate. The vibrations are then transmitted by the bones of the middle ear to the cochlea of the inner ear where they activate tiny sensory hairs which send electrical signals to the brain. The brain translates these into sounds which we can then understand and respond to.

The middle ear also contains the semi-circular canals, the organ we rely on to maintain balance. As we move, the fluid in this organ swirls around which activates sensors that send messages to the brain about the position of the body.

The sense of smell is the one we use the least, but which probably has the biggest subconscious effect on us. Inside the nose are two small patches of tissue called the olfactory membranes. When we breathe in some of the air passes over the sensory cells in these membranes, triggering electrical impulses which travel along nerves directly to the brain. When we have a cold, mucus in our nose prevents odours from reaching the olfactory membrane so we will have difficulty detecting smells and tastes.

The surface of the tongue is covered by tiny projections called papillae which contain taste buds to help us to distinguish between sweet, sour, salty or bitter tastes. Sense organs on the tongue and lips respond to touch and to different textures.

Nerve endings in the skin which respond to touch are unevenly distributed over the body, with the skin of the face and head being far more sensitive than the skin of the feet. These same sensory nerve endings are the ones which enable us to feel pain. When we step on something sharp, messages are sent along the nerves via the spinal cord to the brain. In the spinal cord some of this information is processed and sent back down the motor nerves of the leg to the foot. This reflex reaction makes the muscles of the leg contract, lifting up the foot and rapidly removing it from danger. The messages that pass to the brain tell us that we have hurt ourselves. Rubbing helps to make the pain go away because it cuts off some of the pain sensations.

Thermoreceptors in the skin react to hot and cold, sending messages to the brain to adjust the temperature of the body. When we are cold the blood supply to the skin is restricted to cut down heat loss. This makes the fingernails and lips turn blue and the skin around our hair follicles contract, making goose bumps appear. When we get too hot the blood flow to the skin increases so we appear red and warm. The body also starts to sweat so that the evaporation of water from the surface of the skin cools it down.

Digestive system

In the digestive system food is progressively broken down to provide the energy and nutrients we need for movement and growth. In the mouth food is chewed and chopped by the teeth to break it into smaller pieces and enzymes in our saliva will start to break down sugary and starchy foods.

Bacteria in the mouth also break down sugars to produce acid which can attack the enamel layer on the outside of the teeth, causing the teeth to rot. Regular tooth brushing cuts down the number of bacteria in the mouth and removes food debris.

When food is swallowed it passes down the oesophagus and into the stomach. Here it is churned by the contraction of the muscles in the stomach wall and mixed with gastric juices containing enzymes which will start to break down protein.

The food then passes into the small intestine where bile is added from the gall bladder to break down globules of fat into smaller droplets. Further enzymes are added to the food mixture to continue the breakdown of starch into sugars, fat into fatty acids and protein into amino acids.

The lower part of the small intestine is covered in millions of tiny finger-like projections known as villi. This is where glucose, fatty acids, glycerol and amino acids pass through the walls of the villi into the bloodstream before they are carried round the body to provide a source of energy and nutrients for the cells. Any material not absorbed in the villi will continue to move through the small intestine until it reaches the colon. In the colon water is reabsorbed into the body and any remaining undigested material becomes more solid as it forms into faeces. Faeces are stored temporarily in the rectum until they pass out of the body through the anus.

Reproductive and endocrine systems

The male reproductive organs, the testicles and the penis, are on the outside of the body. Sperm are manufactured in the cells of the testicles from puberty onwards, under the influence of the hormones produced by the endocrine system, particularly testosterone. The female reproductive system is made up of the ovaries, fallopian tubes, uterus, cervix and vagina. Ovulation occurs approximately once per month from puberty through to the menopause, when a mature egg is shed from the ovary into the fallopian tube. Ovulation is influenced by hormones from the endocrine system, particularly oestrogen and progesterone. If an egg is fertilized by a single sperm from the male it develops into a foetus, if not it passes out of the body during menstruation.

Conception occurs when a sperm cell produced by the male comes in contact with an egg in the fallopian tubule of the female. The sperm cell penetrates the egg and the contents of the two cells combine together.

Only the strongest sperm will survive the long journey to the site of the mature egg, helping to ensure that only the best genetic material is passed on to the next generation. Identical twins form if a fertilized egg splits into two before starting to grow in the uterus. Non-identical twins develop if two eggs are released at ovulation and these are then fertilized by two different sperm.

The reproductive cells, the egg and the sperm, each contain 23 unpaired chromosomes. When the sperm and egg come together at fertilization the new cell which forms has a full complement of 46 chromosomes – 23 chromosomes from the mother and 23 from the father. The characteristics which the baby is born with are inherited from both of the parents and carried in the genes located on chromosomes inside the cells of the body. The information in the genes determines physical characteristics such as hair colour, skin tone and eye colour and these are influenced by a combination of genes working together.

In the male and the female sex cells, the sperm and the egg, 22 of the chromosomes are identical in size and structure, but one pair, the X and Y chromosomes, will be different. All female cells contain a pair of X chromosomes, so every egg contains one X chromosome. In males the chromosome pair is made up of one X chromosome and one Y chromosome so sperm can contain either the X or Y member of this pair. If a sperm containing an X chromosome fertilizes an egg the new chromosome pair is XX and so the baby will be female. If a sperm carrying a Y chromosome fertilizes the egg the chromosome pairing will be XY and so the baby will be male.

The endocrine system is responsible for producing the hormones which affect physical characteristics and sexual maturation. Most act on the body over a long period of time, but one of these chemicals, adrenaline, causes a very rapid response to danger by preparing the body to react quickly. The release of adrenaline dilates the pupils of the eye, diverts blood flow to the muscles, speeds up the heart so it pumps more blood to the muscles, expands the lungs to take in more oxygen and makes the liver release blood sugar and fats to provide energy. All these reactions prime the body for action in response to danger.

Healthy living

Living a healthy lifestyle involves feeling both physically and emotionally well. Physical wellbeing is achieved by eating a healthy diet and taking regular exercise. Emotional wellbeing comes from feeling physically safe and secure, having a positive self-image and sense of self-worth and from being a participant in secure loving relationships.

- *Healthy eating*
  Food provides the body with the energy it needs to stay alive. This energy keeps the vital organs of the body functioning, makes the muscles of the body contract so it can move, is used for growth and repair and keeps the body warm. A healthy diet contains the correct balance of carbohydrates, protein, fat and small amounts of essential vitamins and minerals, sufficient fibre to keep the digestive system working well and enough water to ensure that the cells of the body do not become dehydrated.
  Healthy eating contributes to:

  o health, wellbeing and the ability to learn;
  o growth and physical development;
  o the prevention of childhood diseases;
  o protection against diseases later in life;
  o providing the energy needed to enjoy life.

- *Exercise*
  Exercise contributes to the healthy development of bones and muscles, minimizes the risk factors for the development of high blood pressure and helps to increase the mineral density of the bones. Exercise is the basis of energy balance and weight control and contributes to a feeling of personal wellbeing. Regular physical activity:

  o maintains muscle strength and slows down muscle decay;
  o strengthens the muscles of the heart;
  o increases the number of blood vessels in the muscles so they can work more effectively.

The body also needs regular periods of rest and sleep in order to function well. During sleep the brain stores new information through a process known as memory consolidation. Lack of sleep makes people irritable and unable to concentrate and more prone to accidents.

- *Emotional wellbeing*
  Emotional wellbeing and security depend on the interactions which we have with the environment and the relationships we establish with people around us. Young children experience the world around them with all their senses and the environment they grow up in has an enormous influence on them. Scent, sound, texture, light, colour and taste are all sensations which help to create the emotional backdrop against which social and intellectual development take place.
  For young children, strong positive relationships with parents and carers help to fulfil their emotional need for comfort, affection, respect and approval. When these needs are met a young child develops emotional security and sees himself as competent and confident, able to tackle

challenges and solve problems for himself. Emotionally secure children are resilient – they are willing to keep trying things until they are successful.

Both nature and nurture have a significant influence on young children's developing sense of self. The brains of boys and girls show some differences, but there are far more similarities than there are differences. Part of the reason why boys and girls behave differently is determined by the biology of the brain, including the effects of hormones and part by the experiences which young children are exposed to.

Sexual differentiation begins in the womb during the early stages of development of the foetus. Boy and girl babies are born with slightly different mental skills and emotional attitudes which then influence the types of activities they prefer. On average, females are more inclined towards 'social activities' and boys prefer activities which involve movement and spatial awareness.

At the age of two to three toddlers will imitate what they perceive as gender appropriate behaviour, meaning that girls will tend to copy the role model provided by their mother and boys the role model provided by their father. These gender differences are reinforced by the expectations adults have of boys and girls. For example, we often use different words when talking about boy babies and girl babies and the different types of toys which toddlers and young children play with reinforce these distinctions.

Contexts for learning about the human body and healthy living

Babies

Exploring their bodies and finding out a little about how they work helps babies to gain mastery over themselves as they interact with their immediate environment. They will be **observing closely, following instructions, recalling** what has happened in the past, **making predictions** and **trying out ideas**.

>> **Name and sing**

Use this activity to help babies gain an awareness of their bodies, and to hear and learn the names of various body parts.

With the youngest babies, spend time stroking their toes, repeating the word 'toe' as you touch their toes. Now do the same with different part of the body:

| nose | cheek | finger | hair |

Then try singing this song to the tune of 'London Bridge is Falling Down'. Take the baby's hand and pointing to the parts of her body as you sing:

> I can touch my chin, chin, chin
> Chin, chin, chin
> I can touch my chin, chin, chin
> Clever baby

Repeat the song, using other parts of the body:

> I can touch my nose, nose, nose
> I can touch my hand, hand, hand
> I can touch my knees, knees, knees

Try singing and naming the parts of the baby's body in front of a mirror.

Observe:

- How the baby **concentrates** on what you are saying.
- How she **mimics** your actions.
- How she begins to **predict** what is going to happen next.
- How she demonstrates her **curiosity** about what is happening.

›› Find the fruit

As you talk to the babies you will be able to give very positive messages about the fruit and healthy snacks you are hiding and finding.

Talk to the baby as you put him into a highchair and wash his hands. Show him a banana as you cut it into pieces. Make encouraging noises about how nice the banana will be for a snack.

With the baby watching, hide a piece of banana under a clear plastic beaker and encourage the baby to look for it and to take it to eat.

Play the game several times until the baby is finding the prize confidently.

Now try hiding the banana under a coloured tumbler and encourage the baby to look for it. You can make the game more complex by using more than one beaker.

Observe:

- How **interested** he is in finding the banana.
- How he **manipulates** the beaker.
- The **length of time** he persists in playing the game.
- How he **uses prior knowledge** to **predict** what will happen next.

Snapshot

Kyle and his key person are sitting in front of a mirror. She is talking about parts of the body and he is mimicking her actions as she pulls faces and moves her arms around.

Kyle is learning to recognize and name parts of his body and is discovering that some materials reflect light.

Toddlers

By developing their **physical coordination skills** children become **increasingly independent** as their experience and mastery of the world around them grow. Their **small and large motor skills** develop, along with their **concentration** and **reasoning skills**.

>> Follow me

'Follow-my-leader' action games help children to recognize the different parts of their bodies and what they can do.

Show the children how to find a clear space around them and explain that they are going to watch you, as the leader, and copy your actions. Now do the appropriate actions as you say:

'Clap your hands.'
'Stamp your feet.'
'Put your hands on your head.'
'Touch your nose.'
'Stand on one leg.'

Encourage the children to copy your actions.

Introduce the children to the action song 'Heads and Shoulders, Knees and Toes'. Sit in a circle with the children and sing the first verse of the song, pointing to the parts of the body as you sing them:

Heads and shoulders, knees and toes,
Knees and toes.
Heads and shoulders, knees and toes,
Knees and toes.
And eyes and ears and mouth and nose.
Heads and shoulders, knees and toes,
Knees and toes.

Sing the verse again with the children joining in.

In the second verse point to your head but do not say 'head'.

In the third verse point to your head and shoulders without saying the words.

Carry on throughout the song until you are pointing to the parts of the body without saying the words at all.

Finish by singing the whole song as quickly as the children can manage.

This will take some time for the children to master so it is worth repeating the game regularly.

Observe:

- How well they **concentrate** to follow the sequence of the song.
- How the children **cooperate** and **learn from one another**.
- How they **organize information** and **follow instructions**.

>> Good shot

Working with an individual child, place a laundry basket or large container at a distance which is likely to lead to success for the child.

Take turns throwing a variety of objects into the basket. Try:

- different balls – a rubber ball, a hollow ball or a table tennis ball;
- a few scarves – try them flat and rolled up;
- scrunched up paper;
- wooden and plastic clothes pegs.

Use the throwing game as an opportunity to practise counting. As you prepare to throw say 'One, two, three go!' You can also count the objects you have thrown.

Try extending the activity by putting objects of different weights into socks and tying knots in the socks. The children will need to work out how best to throw the different socks.

Observe:

- How different children **coordinate their actions** and develop their motor skills.
- How children use prior knowledge to **solve problems** and **overcome challenges**.
- How **persistent** and **resilient** individual children are.

Preschool children

Finding out more about 'ourselves', the features and characteristics of human beings, how we change as we grow and how our body works will help to build young children's self-awareness and sense of identity. There will be opportunities to **observe closely, compare and contrast, share ideas, record information** and learn about **cause and effect**.

>> Growing up

This is an opportunity to look at how humans grow and change as they get older. It will help children to appreciate change over time and may create opportunities to talk sensitively about birth and death.

What you need:

- Photos of the children in your setting as babies.
- Photos of the children's family members – try to include parents, brothers, sisters and other family members.
- Collection of baby clothes, shoes and toys.
- Height chart or measuring stick.
- Digital camera.

What to do:

Ask the children's parents to provide some pictures of the children when they were babies and toddlers. You could add some of your own!

Look at the photographs with the children and help them to put the photographs in sequence.

- What are the people in the photographs wearing?
- What are they doing?
- Are they lying down, sitting up or moving around?

Talk with the children about how their height has changed as they have grown older. Look at the sizes of hands and feet in the photographs. Talk about 'growing out' of clothes and shoes and illustrate this with examples of baby clothes.

Set up a measuring chart in your setting. Help to organize height measuring sessions at regular intervals during the year so that children can see how much they have grown.

Talk about what babies, children and adults are able to do. Ask the children if they can remember what they could do at different ages.

Draw attention to what the children can already do, what they are almost able to do and what they will be able to do when they are older.

Take some individual photographs of the children in your setting – if you have a digital camera you could encourage the children to take these pictures themselves.

Look at the pictures with the children, helping them to notice similarities and differences.

This is a good opportunity to make a 'Can Do' chart for each child, emphasizing their competencies. The chart could be part of a personal book in which each child includes his or her photographs.

You could also arrange visits from a parent with a new baby or a health visitor. Try recreating the health visitor's clinic in your role play area.

Observe:

- How **interested** the children are in the photographs and the comments they make.
- How they **reflect** on things that have happened in the past.
- The way in which they **organize and record information**.
- The words they use to **describe similarities and differences**.

>> All puffed out

What you need:

- Space to run, dance or jump around vigorously.
- Simple picture books of the human body showing the position of the heart and the lungs.
- A stethoscope – the toy stethoscopes in children's doctors' kits work surprisingly well.

What to do:

Look at the picture books with the children and help them to identify the different parts of the body.

Encourage them to sit as still as possible and then ask:

- What can you feel if you put your hands on your chest and press gently?
- Is there a part of your body that is still moving?

Encourage them to take a few deep breaths in and out and feel their chests moving up and down.

Now run, jump or dance energetically for one minute and then stop.

Ask them:

- Can you notice anything different about your breathing?
- Do you feel your heart beating?

Use the stethoscope to help the children hear the sounds of their hearts beating and their lungs breathing.

If you repeat these bursts of activity several times you will be able to draw children's attention to the other effects of exercise – getting hotter, going red in the face, sweating and getting tired.

Use this as an opportunity to talk to the children about the importance to all of us to take regular exercise in order to keep our hearts and lungs healthy.

Observe:

- How the children **follow instructions**.
- The words they use to **describe** what is happening.
- Any **suggestions they put forward** to explain what is happening.
- How they **handle and manipulate** the tools.

Developing effective scientific communication

Helping children to learn more about their bodies and how they work will enable them to take increasing responsibility for their own health and wellbeing. Knowing the correct words to use will build children's self-confidence and ability to express their ideas, thoughts and feelings.

baby	toddler	child	teenager
adult	young	old	small
big	bigger	mother	father
clothes	shoes	tall	grow
body	head	arm	leg
shoulder	hand	finger	foot
toe	joint	knee	elbow
ankle	face	ear	eye
nose	mouth	stomach	heart
lungs	bone	rib	skeleton

Children will enjoy talking about themselves, what they can do and how they are different from one another. As they do so they will come up with all sorts of interesting ideas which you could explore further.

Other possibilities to investigate include:

- Can you hear better with your eyes closed?
- Do the smallest people have the biggest hands?
- Who can jump further, a boy or a girl?
- Do taller people have longer arms that shorter people?
- Do we all have the same shaped ears?

Equipment and resources

Children under 3

Large wooden hand lens
Sheet magnifiers
Large stand magnifier
Small mirrors
Large mirror equipment – Mirror exploratory and Kaleidoscope mirror
Torches
Wind chimes
Percussion frog
Shakers and castanets
Small world characters e.g. Tolo First Friends
Tolo: Healthy Eating Chef Character Puppet
Tolo: Hospital Bear Character Puppet
Collections of fabrics and materials with different textures
Good quality wooden fruit and vegetables
Laminated photographs of food, physical activity, emotions
Picture books, rhymes and stories about growing up, families, feelings and
    emotions
Action songs and rhymes

3 to 5 year olds

Magnifiers and hand lenses
Sheet magnifiers
Large stand magnifier
Hand-held mirrors
Large mirror equipment – Mirror exploratory and Kaleidoscope mirror
Torches
Wind chimes
Human X-rays
Zac's bones (*Reflections on Learning: www.reflectionsonlearning.co.uk*)

Stethoscope
Cooking utensils
Resources for physical play outdoors – bean bags, hoops, skittles, streamers
Small world characters e.g. Tolo First Friends
Tolo: Healthy Eating Chef Character Puppet
Tolo: Hospital Bear Character Puppet
Laminated photographs of food, physical activity, emotions
Picture books, rhymes and stories about growing up, families, feelings and
    emotions
Action songs and rhymes

Further reading

Brunton, P. and Thornton, L. (2006) *Little Book of Living Things*. Lutterworth: Featherstone
    Education.
Brunton, P. and Thornton, L. (2009) *Healthy Living in the Early Years Foundation Stage*.
    London: Optimus.
Walker, R. (2005) *Dorling Kindersley Guide to the Human Body*. London: Dorling
    Kindersley.

6   **Materials**

Chapter Summary

This chapter reviews the different ways in which materials can be sorted and classified and looks in a little more detail at the particulate theory of matter which explains why things exist as solids, liquids or gases. It looks at how materials change from one state to another and describes why some of these changes are reversible and some are not. This provides the context for exploring materials with young children through the use of a Treasure Basket, finding out about fabrics, investigating mixtures, and experiencing what happens to ice when the temperature rises. The uses to which different materials can be put are explored along with an everyday example of chemical change.

Background knowledge

Sorting and classifying materials

The term 'materials' is used to describe all the different things – the 'stuff' – that the world is made of. These include metal, plastic, wood, paper, glass, rock, water, air. Everything, including us, the clothes we wear and the food we eat, can be described as materials. Different materials have different properties and behave in different ways – they can be hard, soft, rough, smooth, heavy, light, springy, firm, shiny or dull. Some materials can be changed from one form to another. We experience examples of materials changing when we stir sugar into a cup of tea, make toast, bake a cake or drop ice cubes into a drink.

Materials can be classified in many different ways depending on the criteria you choose.

Common ways of sorting materials include:

- dividing them into those that normally exist as solids, liquids or gases;
- separating them into natural and manufactured materials;
- classifying them by their properties and what they are used for.

Solids, liquids and gases

Everything in the world around us is made of very small units called particles. How these particles are arranged determines whether something is a solid, a liquid or a gas. These three different forms which materials can take are known as the states of matter.

- *Solids*
  If the particles in a material are held together closely, linked to one another and not able to move apart, the material will be a solid. Solids have a fixed volume and shape, although they will vary in hardness from very soft materials like sponge or cotton wool to very hard materials like rock or iron. Some solids, like sand or flour, can be poured like liquids because they are made up of very small pieces of solid material. When sand is poured into a container it forms a pointed cone shape rather than the flat surface that a liquid has.
- *Liquids*
  If the particles in a material are further apart, so that they can move around more, the material will be a liquid. Liquids have a fixed volume but not a fixed shape. They take the shape of the container they are in and flow in a downward direction. Some liquids can be very thick and viscous, like syrup or engine oil, and flow very slowly. Water is the liquid which we are most familiar with and is essential for all life on Earth (see Chapter 8).

  Not all liquids mix with one another – oil and water do not mix, but instead form two separate layers with the oil layer floating on top of the water layer. We notice this when we see a rainbow effect on the surface of an oily puddle of water. Liquids are hard to compress, a phenomenon we make use of in hydraulics (see Chapter 8).
- *Gases*
  If the particles in a material are even more widely spaced and are able to move around freely, the material will be a gas. Gases have no fixed shape or volume and the individual particles of the gas move to fill the space available to them. This is how smells are transmitted from one place to another. Air is an example of a mixture of gases, largely nitrogen and oxygen (see Chapter 8). Because the gas particles are relatively far apart from one another they can be compressed into a smaller space fairly easily. We make use of this property of gases when we inflate a tyre or a balloon or use pneumatics to make something move (see Chapter 8).

Natural and manufactured materials

This would appear at first sight to be a simple way to classify materials into two groups – those that occur naturally in the world and those that have been 'made'.

Wood, rock, sand and wool are all examples of natural materials. However, when we experience these materials they have often been changed in some way:

- tree trunks are cut and sanded and shaped into planks of wood, chairs and tables;
- rock is cut, crushed or shaped into building materials and slate;
- sand is mixed with stones and cement to form concrete;
- wool, silk and cotton are washed, processed and spun into yarn or thread.

Manufactured materials include all those that have been produced by human ingenuity using a range of naturally occurring resources. The two major groups are:

- plastics which are made from oil – these exist in many different forms and can be hard or soft, transparent or opaque, flexible or rigid;
- metals that are produced by heating and smelting rocks – some of these, such as gold and silver are very rare and expensive, while others including iron and aluminium are more common: many metals can be combined together to make alloys such as brass, zinc and stainless steel.

Classifying materials by their properties and use

Classifying materials by their properties and how they are used is an excellent way to help young children extend their understanding of materials. It is easier for them to classify materials in this way as it makes use of properties that they can feel and see rather than theoretical knowledge.

From your own experience of materials you will be aware of the following.

- Metals are often hard and feel cold. An object made of metal will feel heavy (although aluminium is very light), will conduct electricity and will make a 'metallic' ringing sound if you hit it. Some metals have shiny surfaces which reflect light and act as mirrors.
- Wood is strong and flexible and made of fibres. Objects made of wood can be heavy or light, they usually float in water and can be cut with a saw and sanded smooth.

- Plastics are light and very long lasting. They can be bent and stretched, cut and shaped. Plastic objects don't conduct electricity and usually float in water.
- Glass lets light pass through it. Glass breaks easily and when it is heated it can be blown and moulded into different shapes.

Change of state

Some materials are very versatile and can exist as solids, liquids or gases. Water is a good example of this. At very low temperatures, below 0° C, water is a solid; between 0° and 100° C water exists as a liquid; above 100° C it turns into a gas.

When a solid is heated, the heat energy makes the particles vibrate more rapidly. As the particles gain enough energy to break free from one another the solid melts and becomes a liquid. The temperature at which this happens is called the melting point of the solid. For ice this is 0° C. If the heating continues, the particles vibrate more and more rapidly until they move away from one another sufficiently to become a gas. This is the boiling point of the liquid, which for water is 100° C.

Evaporation and condensation

When water evaporates – for example from the surface of a puddle on a sunny day – it changes from a liquid to a gas called water vapour. When the sun shines on the puddle it warms up the water, giving the water molecules more energy so they move around faster and escape from the surface as vapour. The hotter the day, the faster this process takes place and the quicker the puddle will dry up.

Condensation is the reverse of the evaporation process. As the temperature falls the gas particles vibrate less so they come closer together until they reform into a liquid. If the temperature falls even further the vibration of the liquid particles will slow down until eventually they will freeze into a solid.

Physical and chemical change

The wide range of changes which different materials can undergo is divided into two broad categories – physical change and chemical change. Physical change happens when a material is converted from one form to another, for example from a solid to a liquid. Physical changes are usually reversible: the material can be changed back again to a solid just by changing the conditions.

Chemical change of a material alters the structure of the material in some way, resulting in the creation of something new. For this reason chemical change is permanent and not reversible.

Physical change

When materials are changed physically the individual particles that they are made up of remain the same, they are just arranged in a different way. Evaporation and condensation, and ice melting and turning from a solid to a liquid, are each examples of physical change. If we collect liquid water and put it back into the freezer we can convert it back into solid ice again.

Adding sugar to water is an interesting example of a physical change. When the solid sugar is stirred into the water it seems to disappear. We can establish that it is still there because if we taste the water it will be sweet. What has happened is that the crystals of sugar have broken down in the water and the tiny individual sugar molecules have dispersed throughout the water creating a sugar solution. The sugar is still there and can be recovered by leaving the solution exposed to the air, in a warm place, for a few days. Over time the water will evaporate from the surface of the solution and the sugar crystals will begin to crystallize into a solid again.

Chemical change

Chemical change is not reversible. It results in the creation of something new which is different from the original material. Common examples of chemical change include burning and cooking.

- *Burning*
  When materials burn they undergo a chemical change. For example, when bread is put in a toaster water is lost and the carbohydrate on the surface of the bread changes colour and is converted to carbon.

  When a candle burns, the wax melts to form a liquid and then converts to a gas as it burns in the candle flame. As it burns, the gas changes to water and carbon dioxide while at the same time releasing energy as heat and light.

- *Cooking*
  Most of the changes which take place during cooking are examples of irreversible chemical change. For example, when eggs, sugar, flour and butter are combined together to make a cake and then put in the oven the sloppy mixture is converted into a solid which is firm and retains its shape. All of the ingredients have been chemically changed by combining with one another and then by being heated to a high temperature.

Contexts for learning about materials

Babies

Exploring materials gives young babies the opportunity to **satisfy their curiosity** about the world around them. They will be **using all their senses** to **explore** and will be building up the experience they need to **sort and classify**. In finding out **how different materials behave** they will be developing their **manipulative skills** and gaining **first-hand** experience of how simple tools work.

≫ Exploring a Treasure Basket

A Treasure Basket is a low wicker basket, approximately 12 centimetres high and 30 centimetres in diameter, filled with 80–100 different objects made from wood, metal, glass, card and natural materials. It is for use with non-mobile babies to enable them to find out what different objects feel like, taste like, sound like and look like. Through this process they will build their understanding of what different materials are like – how heavy or light, rough or smooth they are and how they behave when they are picked up, waved about, banged together or put down.

Observe:

- Which objects the baby is particularly **interested** in.
- How the baby **manipulates** the objects.
- How the baby **uses her senses to investigate** the objects to find out what they will do.
- **How long** the baby **concentrates** on using the Treasure Basket.

>> Fabric fun

Put together a collection of different fabrics for the babies to explore. Include:

- fine, lightweight fabrics such as muslin or voile;
- heavy fabrics such as corduroy and canvas;
- cotton and nylon;
- interesting textures such as fur fabric and fabrics with a metallic finish;
- knitted fabrics which have interesting surface textures and can stretch;
- elasticized materials;
- rubberized and waterproof materials;
- leather and PVC.

Sit with the babies and investigate the fabrics together. Talk to them about:

- how rough or smooth the textures feel;
- how warm or cold they are to touch;
- which ones are heavy and which are light;
- which ones you can see through;
- which ones stretch.

Encourage them to explore what they can do with the fabrics.

Observe:

- How **curious** the babies are about the fabrics.
- How they **make choices** and **express their preferences**.
- The different ways they **explore** the fabrics.
- What they choose to do with them and how they find out **how things behave**.

Snapshot

Kim and Nazim sit side by side investigating a basket of brushes. Nazim lifts out a make-up brush with a soft head and brushes the back of his hand. He smiles and starts to stroke his cheek with the brush. Kim sees what he is doing and copies his actions using the nail brush she is holding. She looks very surprised when she discovers what the brush feels like on her face.

Kim and Nazim are learning about how materials differ from one another and about how simple tools work.

Toddlers

While investigating materials young children will be learning to **compare and contrast, sort and classify** in order to develop the ideas they are exploring. They will be finding out how materials behave in different situations and beginning to see the association between **cause and effect**.

>> ### Exploring mixtures

Exploring how different materials behave when they are mixed together gives toddlers an early understanding of how different things react with one another as part of the processes of physical and chemical change.

Provide a collection of bowls and wooden spoons and a range of different materials which can be mixed together. These could include flour, sand, water, rice, dried beans, small pebbles, cooked pasta, cornflour.

Encourage the children to choose different materials to mix together to explore what happens. Some children will use spoons while others will prefer to use their hands.

Talk about the changes you can see happening as more or different ingredients are added to the mixture. Talk about what things look like, feel like and smell like.

Encourage the children to look closely at what happens when water is added to flour or to cornflour.

Observe:

- How **confident** individual children are in investigating the mixtures.
- The **choices** children make when creating their mixtures.
- How they **manipulate** the tools they use.
- Any **comments and observations** they make about what things look like, feel like, smell like or sound like.

>> ### Ice stories

This is an opportunity to investigate change of state and to build on what children already know about ice and how it behaves. Set up a large tray, either indoors or out of doors, adding ice cubes and some water. If you are making your own ice cubes, you could add blue food colouring to the water before freezing it.

Encourage the children to create an imaginary world with the ice, water and some small world play resources. Talk about what the ice feels like, what it sounds like and what is happening to it over time. Blue ice cubes will very obviously be changing; the coloured ice will have a very visual effect as it melts and changes the colour of the water already in the tray.

When the children have finished playing with the ice cubes, look at how much water there now is in the tray. Talk to them about what they think would happen if they put the water back into a freezer. Re-freeze the water using balloons or rubber gloves as moulds and have more fun.

Observe:

- How **confident** the children are in handling the resources.
- How **curious** they are about what is happening to the ice.
- Any **ideas they suggest** about where the ice has gone.
- Any **suggestions they make** about how to stop the ice melting.

Preschool children

Building on their previous experience of materials and how they behave children will be **sorting and classifying**, and **recalling what they already know** about how different materials are used. They will be **using their senses, following instructions** and **finding out information**.

>> **The builders' yard**

What you need:

- A large plastic tool box containing a selection of building materials and tools which are safe for children to handle.
- This could include off-cuts of wood, plastic drain pipes, metal brackets, paintbrushes, a measuring tape, spirit level, hard hat, safely goggles.

What to do:

Leave the tool box and the building materials in a suitable place outside for the children to find them. When they discover the box encourage them to investigate it carefully.

Discuss all the different tools and materials they find.

- What do you think they are used for?
- What are they made of?
- Has anyone seen one of these before?
- Do you know how to use it?
- Can you show me?

Help the children to create a builders' yard and talk about how all the different building materials are used.

Go for a 'building walk' inside and outside the setting and see how many different types of building materials the children can spot.

- What do you think they are made of?

Encourage the children to use the correct words to describe the different materials.

Observe:

- How the children **sort and classify** the materials.
- How they **manipulate** the tools.
- How **observant** they are about how different materials are used.
- The **words they use** to describe the different materials they experience.

 ### Snapshot

Chloe tips two cups of cornflour into a shallow tray and then pours in one cup of water. As she mixes the two together with her fingers she describes how the cornflour mixture feels.

'It's all slippery and slimy but it feels very soft on my fingers. I really like it.'

Ricole comes to join her and they explore the mixture together. When she squeezes the mixture Ricole notices that it feels stiff and quite hard.

'Look, it's gone all funny, it isn't soft anymore.'

Their key person joins them in their exploration and together they decide to add some more cornflour to the mixture. Now when they push their fingers quickly through it, it cracks and breaks.

They talk together about what they can see happening and wonder if the same thing will happen if they mix flour and water together.

The girls (and their key person) are discovering that not all materials behave as conventional solids or liquids. Although the cornflour mix behaves at first like a sticky, viscous fluid, when a pressure is applied quickly to the mixture it behaves like a solid for a short time.

>> **Celebration cakes**

What you need:

- The ingredients for making some small cakes – flour, sugar, butter, eggs, milk.
- Mixing bowls and spoons.
- A measuring jug.
- Cake cases and bun tins.
- A recipe book.

What to do:

This is a good opportunity to talk to the children about the importance of washing their hands before starting to cook.

Talk with the children about the different ingredients.

- What do they look like?
- What do they think they will taste like?
- How will everyone know how much of each ingredient to add?

Help the children to measure out the ingredients and begin to mix them together.

Draw their attention to the changes you see happening – solids turning to liquids, solids and liquids combining together.

Discuss what they think will happen when the cake mixture goes into the oven.

Bake the cakes and when they are cool, look at them and then break one open and look inside.

- What shape are the cakes now?
- Are they the same as they were before they went into the oven?
- Can you see the air holes in the cake?
- Can you see eggs or the sugar or the butter inside the cake?

Take photographs throughout the activity so children can reflect on the different stages of the process.

Observe:

- How the children **observe** and describe the different ingredients.
- The **predictions** they make about what will happen to the ingredients.
- How they **follow the instructions** in the recipe.
- The way they **manipulate** the tools.
- The **ideas they put forward** about how the materials have changed.
- Any **explanations** they offer as to why things have happened.

Developing effective scientific communication

Helping children to build a broad vocabulary to describe the many different materials they come across will give them the tools they need to identify, sort and classify-all key scientific skills. The best way to do this is to model the correct use of these words in conversations you have with the children and to reinforce this process through the use of carefully labelled displays, signs and notices.

wood	glass	metal	plastic
stone	shell	fabric	paper
cardboard	rubber	leather	wool
cotton	canvas	hard	soft
rough	smooth	stretchy	stiff
heavy	light	shiny	dull
natural	artificial	sand	water
liquid	solid	gas	air
hot	cold	melt	freeze
ice	change	measure	size
dissolve	stir	pour	shape

Young children's experience of materials can be extended by using the ideas and suggestions that they come up with as starting points for further exploration. This builds on their interests and preoccupations and can lead to some very interesting and unusual investigations.

You could also pose your own questions and challenges to extend children's scientific thinking and reasoning skills.

For example:

- What do you think would happen to an ice balloon if we left it outside in the rain?
- What fabric would be best for making a raincoat for teddy?
- How many different ways could we sort a collection of hats?
- Are all shiny things made of metal?
- Is all glass transparent?

Equipment and resources

Children under 3

Large wooden hand lens
Sheet magnifiers
Large stand magnifier
Large plastic 'discovery' trays
Transparent plastic buckets
Clear plastic beakers and jugs
Jumbo test tubes
Light box
Mirror Exploratory
Colour-changing ducks
Woven wicker baskets
Sisal baskets
Collections of natural materials – leaves, seed pods, wood, shells, stones, sand, wool, leather
Collection of household objects made from metal, wood, plastic, card
Collection of reclaimed materials
Collection of materials from builders' merchants

3 to 5 year olds

Large and small magnifiers
Large stand magnifier
Sheet magnifiers
Small acrylic mirrors
Triptych mirror
Portable light box
Mirrored infinity cubes
Jumbo test tubes
Plastic pipettes
Petri dishes

Collection of natural materials – leaves, seed pods, wood, shells, stones, sand,
   wool, leather
Collection of household objects made from metal, wood, plastic, card
Collection of reclaimed materials
Collection of materials from builders' merchants
Let's Explore: Looking Closely kits (*Reflections on Learning*: *www.
   reflectionsonlearning.co.uk*)

Further reading

Hughes, A. M. (2006) *Developing Play for the Under 3s*. London: David Fulton.
The Oxford Children's Encyclopaedia of Science and Technology (2000) Oxford: Oxford
   University Press.
The Dorling Kindersley Science Encyclopaedia (2004) London: Dorling Kindersley.
Williams, R.A., Rockwell, R.E. and Sherwood, E.A. (1987) *Mudpies to Magnets*.
   Beltsville, MD: Gryphon House.

7 Forces

Chapter Summary

This chapter looks at how forces – pushes and pulls, gravity and friction – affect our everyday lives. It looks at simple machines and how they work and at the science behind springiness and elasticity and the principles behind the action of simple machines. Understanding how forces behave creates a context for helping children to explore the effects of gravity, experience push, pull and twist forces, investigate the effects of forces on malleable materials and feel the effects of friction.

Background knowledge

Pushes and pulls

Forces are all around us – they make things move, change shape and balance. Whatever you are doing in daily life forces will be affecting you, whether opening doors, getting dressed or standing still. Children will experience the forces of push, pull and twist when using puppets, reading pop-up books, performing action rhymes, threading beads, digging and lifting sand, riding bikes, weaving and playing percussion instruments. You can't see forces, only their effects, and some forces can't be felt. This makes them difficult to understand – or believe in!

All forces are either pushes or pulls. A twist is a particular kind of pull or push which involves turning. Forces can make things:

- stay still or start to move;
- speed up or slow down;
- change direction;
- change shape.

The way in which forces affect the movement of objects was summarized by Sir Isaac Newton in his three laws of motion.

- *First law of motion*
  An object remains stationary or moves at a constant speed in a straight line, unless acted on by a resultant force or forces. (For example, a toy car resting on a flat surface stays where it is unless a force is applied to it.)
- *Second law of motion*
  When a force acts on an object the resulting acceleration is directly proportional to the force and inversely proportional to the mass (the amount of matter) of the object. The acceleration changes in the direction the force acts. (For example, pushing a bicycle is easier than pushing a car.)
- *Third law of motion*
  Every action has an equal and opposite reaction. (When a ball hits a wall, the ball exerts a force on the wall and the wall exerts an equal force on the ball in the opposite direction, so the ball bounces off the wall.)

How forces act on objects

- *Staying still and starting to move*
  Objects and people stay still when the forces on them are the same in all directions. A book resting on a table or a person sitting on a chair are pushing downwards with a force; the table and the chair are pushing back with an equal force in the opposite direction. A ball on a flat surface will stay still until a push or a pull is applied to it, when it will start to move. An object floats in water when the forces acting on it are balanced (see Chapter 8).
- *Speeding up and slowing down*
  Forces are being used when an object or a person changes speed – either going faster or slowing down. Pushing yourself along on a scooter will speed you and the scooter up. If you stop pushing, the scooter will slow down and stop.
- *Changing direction*
  You can't change direction without a force. If you push a wheelbarrow or a buggy along in straight line and apply a push or a pull to one of the handles it will change direction. When you roll a ball against a wall it will travel in one direction until it hits the wall. The push from the wall will make it change direction.
- *Changing shape*
  Some objects will change shape when a force is applied to them. Squeezing, squashing and stretching are all terms used to describe push and pull actions. Manipulating dough involves pushing and pulling it to change its shape.

Friction

Friction is a force which affects all types of movement on the Earth. Friction has an effect on the movement of things on the ground, in the air and in water. When two surfaces come into contact with one another there is friction between them. The two surfaces appear to grip onto one another and resist movement. When you walk there is friction between the soles of your shoes and the ground you are walking on. If there wasn't any friction you wouldn't be able to move, your feet would just slip on the surface. A shoe with a rough sole has more friction against a polished floor than a shoe with a smooth sole.

Friction is the force you make use of when you apply the brakes in a car or on a bicycle. Vehicles that move fast along the ground, in the air or through water are designed to be streamlined to cut down the amount of friction – think about the shape of sports cars, racing bikes, jet aircraft and speedboats.

When friction acts between two surfaces some of the energy is given off as heat – rubbing the palms of your hands together to get warm is a good example of this.

Gravity

Gravity is a special kind of force which does not need to touch an object to have its effect. All objects exert a force of gravity but it is only when an object is very large, such as the Earth, that we become aware of this force. The Earth's gravity pulls objects down and holds them on to the Earth. Gravity is acting on us all the time but we are not usually aware of it. If you drop a toy it will always fall downwards due to the pull of gravity. The speed at which the toy falls will be determined by its shape and the amount of air resistance acting on it to slow down its fall (see Chapter 8).

The larger an object the greater the force of gravity it exerts. The force of gravity from the sun keeps the planets in our solar system in orbit around it. The force of gravity of the Earth keeps the moon in orbit around it. As the moon is a smaller object than the Earth the force of gravity it exerts is less – astronauts on the moon can move around much more easily.

Mass and weight

These two terms have very specific scientific meanings. The mass of an object is a measure of the amount of matter in it. This mass doesn't change if an object is on the Earth, in a space rocket or on the moon. Mass is measured in grams and kilograms.

Weight is a measure of the force of gravity acting on an object and is measured in units called newtons. The force of gravity varies depending on where the object is. The same object will weigh less on the moon because the moon is smaller than the Earth so its pull of gravity is less.

In everyday life we use the term 'weight' to apply to the mass of an object and measure this in grams and kilograms, but it is useful to be aware of the difference between the two.

Simple machines

Simple machines such as levers, pulleys, wheels and ramps help us to use forces effectively. They can be used to increase or decrease a force or to change its direction. Levers help to us to do work by transferring the effort from one place to another. When you use a lever to open the lid of a tin, the long push you exert on one end of the lever is transferred to a short upward movement on the lid of the tin. Pulleys help us to lift things by transferring a downward pull on a rope looped over the pulley to an upward force on the object that the rope is attached to.

Springiness and elasticity

When a force acting on an object changes its shape the object will either stay in its new shape or will return to its original shape once the force is removed. Metal springs, which can be squeezed (compressed) or stretched, are a good example of this springiness, or elasticity.

When you squeeze a spring you are using a force to push the coils of the spring closer together so it gets shorter. When you stop pushing the spring, it returns to its original length. We use springs in many different ways to help to make things move, for example, wind-up clocks and clockwork toys, pogo sticks, retractable ballpoint pens and staplers. Springs are also used to absorb forces to help make things more comfortable, such as in a sprung mattress, settees and shock absorbers in cars.

If you pull on a spring it will stretch and become longer as the coils move further apart. When you stop pulling the spring will go back to its original shape. Springs are often used in mechanical weighing scales such as the ones you use for weighing fruit and vegetables in the supermarket. If a spring is stretched too far it will lose its springiness or snap – everything has its 'elastic limit'.

Springs can be used to store energy. When you push down on a jack-in-the-box and close the lid the energy you have used to push it down is stored in the spring. When you open the lid this stored energy is released and the toy pops up.

Springs aren't the only things which stretch and show elasticity. Materials such as rubber, elastic, sponge foam, some types of plastic and dough can all be stretched and squeezed and will then regain their shape once the force is removed.

Contexts for learning about forces

Babies

Exploring forces is an opportunity for babies to gain simple **first-hand experience** of **cause and effect**. There are opportunities for babies to build their **self-confidence** by gaining control over their bodies and to satisfy their **curiosity** by seeing the effect they can have on the world around them.

⟩⟩ Dropping games

Sit a baby up in a highchair and put a selection of different objects on the tray table. These could include a paper tissue, a rubber ball, a wooden block, a piece of bubble plastic, a metal teaspoon.

Pick up one of the objects and talk to the baby about what it feels like and what it looks like.

- I wonder what will happen if I let this go?

Let the object fall out of your hand and draw the baby's attention to what happens to is when it falls.

- Where has it gone?
- Has it fallen down?

Encourage the baby to explore dropping the objects herself. Talk about how the different objects fall and the noise they make when they hit the ground.

- Do any of the objects bounce or roll away?

Observe:

- How **curious** the baby is about what is happening to the objects.
- The **manipulative skills** demonstrated when handling the objects.
- How the baby **makes predictions** about what will happen.
- How often the investigation is repeated to **test these predictions**.

⟩⟩ Row the boat

Sit on the floor opposite a baby. Gently hold on to his hands and start to move him backwards and forwards while singing:

Pull, pull, pull and push,
Back and forth we go ...
Happily, happily, happily, happily,
Pull me if you can.

Emphasize the pull and push movements as you do this.

Now try playing a pulling game with the baby using a scarf. Hold one end of the scarf and give the baby the other end to hold on to. Pull gently on the scarf so the baby's body leans towards you. Repeat this a few times then stop pulling and ask:

• Can you pull me?

Encourage the baby to pull on his end of the scarf and lean forward as he does this.

Talk to him all the time about the pulling actions.

Observe:

• How **interested** he is in the game.
• How easily he **follows simple instructions**.
• How quickly he begins to mimic your actions.
• How well he coordinates his body.

 Snapshot

Jasmine is pushing a large wooden block rapidly across the wooden floor. When she reaches the carpeted area the block becomes much more difficult to move. Her key person is alongside her, commenting on what Jasmine is doing. Jasmine is learning through first-hand experience how the force of push can make things move and how the force of friction can slow things down.

Toddlers

These simple explorations can give toddlers an opportunity to **look closely** at shapes, satisfy their **curiosity** about how things behave and try out their ideas as they **investigate** some simple properties of materials.

>> **Rolling down the hill**

Make a collection of interesting objects that roll. Include balls of different sizes made of different materials, and also include some more unusual 'rolling objects' such as a potato, butternut squash, turnip, gourd, parsnip and carrot.

Encourage the children to explore the 'rolling collection'.

- Which ones do you think will be good at rolling downhill?

Set up a short slope using a piece of wood and a large wooden block. Encourage the children to roll things down the slope.

- Which do you think are the best rollers?
- Which ones roll in a funny way?

Observe:

- How the children **explore** the rolling collection and how they **describe** the objects in it.
- How they **predict** which will be the best rollers.
- How they **test their ideas**.
- How they **sort and classify** the objects in the collection.

>> **Exploring clay**

Working with a group of four to six children, investigate what happens to clay when forces are applied to it.

Keep the clay in a large lump at first and encourage the toddlers to explore it just with their hands. Let them see what sort of marks they can make in the clay with their hands, fingers, arms, elbows (and feet). Talk about pushing and pulling, poking and prodding, twisting and tearing.

Draw the children's attention to the movements involved in each of these actions and to the energy they are expending as they manipulate the clay.

Now divide the large lump up and encourage the children to explore what they can do with the clay – pulling it, pushing it, squeezing, squashing and flattening it.

Introduce some tools and simple machines such as a rolling pin, a garlic press or potato ricer, cutters, lolly sticks, spatulas or clay working tools.

Talk about how these tools work as the children pull, twist, flatten, squash, squeeze, cut and scrape the clay.

Observe:

- How **confidently** the children **explore** the clay.
- How they **use the tools**.
- **How long they persist** in shaping and manipulating the clay.
- How they **describe** what they are doing.

 ## Snapshot

Mai-Yin is intrigued by a collection of large nuts and bolts, some made of metal and others of plastic. Every day she gets the collection out and spends long periods of time fitting the pieces together, showing great pleasure every time she manages to twist a bolt through the correct size nut. She delights in showing other children how to fit the nuts and bolts together.

Mai-Yin is learning about push, pull and twist forces and discovering the pleasure of being able to share her skills with others.

Preschool children

These ideas can help children to build on their previous experiences of forces, to **suggest ideas, plan simple investigations, observe carefully** and **describe what they have discovered.** There are opportunities to **make and test predictions** and **modify ideas in the light of evidence.** Adults can support these processes by giving children **time to explore and investigate** and by encouraging them to **look carefully at**, and **talk about**, what they can see happening.

 ### Balls and ball games

With these games you can explore the effects of gravity, staying still and starting to move, speeding up and slowing down and changing direction.

What you need:

- A hard surfaced outdoor area with a wall or solid fence.
- A slope or ramp – either a permanent feature or a wide plank and some large blocks.
- A set of small balls that are all the same, such as tennis balls or rubber balls.

What to do:

Ask the children to hold a ball in their hands and investigate what happens when they let go of it. Focus the discussion on the balls always falling downwards when they are dropped.

- Can you make a ball fall upwards?

Ask the children to put their balls down on a flat surface.

- Do they move?
- Why not?

Next, explain to the children that you want them to find different ways to make their balls move. Give them time to explore pushing, rolling, kicking, throwing, bouncing and hitting.

- How many different ways did we find to make the balls move?
- Which worked best?
- What does 'best' mean – faster, slower, further, in a straight line?
- If we used a different type of ball do you think we would get the same result?

Observe:

- How individual children **follow instructions**.
- The **ideas** they suggest.
- How they **tested** their ideas.
- How well they **cooperate** with one another.
- How they describe what they have found out.

 ## Snapshot

Jay picks up the Jack-in-the-box and opens the lid. The clown pops up and wobbles around on its spring. Jay pushes down on the clown's head to try to get him back into his box, but can't quite manage it. Tom comes over and shows Jay how to pull on the cord attached to the underside of the box to pull the clown back down. Together they play with the toy, opening and shutting the box and talking about how the clown pops up every time the lid is opened.

The boys are building their understanding of how springs behave and learning how to make use of the forces of push and pull.

>> Feel the friction

This is a chance for a small group of children to investigate the force of friction by pushing a wheeled toy over different surfaces.

What you need:

- Medium-sized wheeled toys such as lorries, tractors or dumper trucks.
- A range of different surfaces to run the toys over, some smooth and some rough – tarmac, grass, sand, concrete, gravel, carpet, lino or wood.

What to do:

Go outside with a small group of children – they will each need a wheeled toy. Look at the different surfaces in your outdoor area and talk about what they feel like – rough, smooth, hard, soft, even or uneven.

- Which surfaces are easiest to walk over?
- Which ones do you think are the most difficult to walk over?

Encourage the children to predict which surfaces the toys will move over easily, and which ones will it will be difficult for the toys to move on. Ask them to give reasons for their predictions.

Let the children explore the different surfaces, testing the ease with which the toys move.

- Which surface is the easiest for the toys to move on?
- Which surface is the most difficult?
- Were your predictions right?
- Did everybody come up with the same result?

Observe:

- The words the children use to **describe** the different outdoor surfaces.
- The **predictions** they make about how well the toys will move.
- The **reasons** they give for these predictions.
- How they decide to **test** the toys.
- How they **describe** what they have discovered.

Developing effective scientific communication

By helping the children to learn the correct terminology to describe different phenomena you will be giving them the tools they need to express their ideas and communicate their discoveries. The accurate use of language is an essential part of expressing scientific ideas in an understandable way.

push	pull	twist	turn
move	squash	squeeze	stretch
poke	pinch	shape	rough
smooth	fast	slow	speed
still	up	down	gravity
friction	grip	slip	spring
elastic	energy	machine	direction

To challenge children's thinking and help them to extend their experience you could pose a range of problems for children to investigate. Many new ideas will arise from the children's interests as revealed during the investigations, but other possibilities could include:

- using a ramp to see how the height of the ramp changes the speed of a rolling ball;
- organizing the children to work in pairs, with one child rolling a ball to make it move and the other child finding a way to slow the ball down or stop it;
- rolling balls against a wall or fence and seeing how they change direction after they touch the wall;
- finding out how far different cars will travel down a wooden ramp;
- discovering which rolls best, an orange or a lemon;
- using a pulley system to move objects from one place to another.

Equipment and resources

Children under 3

Twist 'n' Roll Manipulative toy
Spacy Manipulative toy
Roller Manipulative toy
Cheese Chaser Manipulative toy
Balancing Cactus
Balance Man
(*All from Reflections on Learning: www.reflectionsonlearning.co.uk*)
Large wooden nuts and bolts
Plastic nuts and bolts
Pounding bench
Bead threading sets

Pull-along toys
Large wooden cars and trucks
Wooden building blocks
Large springy toys
Plastic slinky
Collection of balls of different sizes
Collection of rolling things – tubes, gourds, vegetables
Collections of stretchy materials – knitted fabric, rubber, foam, sponge
Nursery rhyme books
Action songs and rhymes

3 to 5 year olds

Large wooden blocks
Ramps and planks
Cars and wheeled vehicles
Marble run
Lego gear set
Jack-in-the-box
Slinky
Press base animals
Pop-up puppets
Clear plastic buckets
Pulley set
Collection of cogs and gears
Collection of kitchen tools including rollers, tongs, garlic press, potato ricer, rotary hand whisk
Bucket balance
Stories and traditional tales involving forces, for example, *The Enormous Turnip*

Further reading

Smith, B. (2004) *The Science You Need to Know.* Hatfield: Association for Science Education.

Stringer, J. (2001) *Teaching the Tricky Bits – Forces, Electricity and Magnetism and the Earth in Space.* London: Hopscotch.

Thornton, L. and Brunton, P. (2006) *Little Book of Treasureboxes.* Lutterworth: Featherstone Education.

8 Air and Water

Chapter Summary

Understanding a little about how air and water behave opens up a wealth of opportunities to explore with young children. This chapter looks at the properties of air, how it can be made to move things and what happens when objects fall through the air. Understanding how water behaves when it is heated or cooled or compressed, when it flows from one place to another, or why some objects will float and some will sink will enable you to extend the opportunities for exploration and investigation presented by the water tray.

Understanding about air provides the context for helping children to explore the movement of air, indoors and out, and to investigate pneumatics. Knowing about the properties of water creates the context for children to find out more about pouring water, using it to make things move, how different materials are affected by water and how to make sinking things float.

Background knowledge

Air

Air is essential for life and while it is all around us we can't see it. However, we can see what it does. We feel the movement of air when we are outside on a windy day, we notice it when we blow bubbles and they drift away and we are aware of it when we make a noise with a whistle or a trumpet.

Air fills the space around us and is the name we give to the mixture of different gases which make up the Earth's atmosphere. Most of the air is made up of the gases nitrogen and oxygen. Oxygen makes up 21 per cent of the air around us and is essential for all living things. When we breathe in, air goes into our lungs. Here oxygen is taken out of the air and this passes into the blood stream. This oxygen then circulates around our bodies and helps to keep us alive (see Chapter 4).

Pneumatics

Making things move by using air is called pneumatics. You can experience pneumatics by squeezing the bulb on a plastic pipette or an empty washing-up liquid bottle and feeling the jet of air which comes out. This jet of air can be used to make ripples on the surface of a bowl of water or to change the shape of a drop of paint on a piece of paper. Blowing down a straw has a similar effect, and if you blow into bubble mixture you can see the air trapped inside the bubbles that form.

Wind

Wind is a current of air moving horizontally across the ground. Winds are caused when air in the atmosphere flows from an area of high pressure to an area of low pressure and can vary in speed from very light breezes to hurricane force winds (see Chapter 14).

Wind is also a source of energy and can make things move by pushing on them. We can feel this push when we are outside on a windy day. The stronger the wind, the greater the force of the push we experience. The bigger the surface area the air pushes against, the greater the force (see Chapter 7). You can experience this on a windy day if you undo your coat, hold on to the sides and spread your arms out.

Wind is used as a source of energy in windmills and in wind turbines. The blades of the turbine or windmill are blown round by the wind and their movement is converted into electricity by a generator (see Chapter 10).

Falling through the air

When things fall through the air they are pulled downwards by the force of gravity (see Chapter 7). As they fall there is friction between the object and the surrounding air. This is called air resistance. Gliders and parachutes make use of air resistance to help them stay airborne and to slow down the rate at which they fall. An object attached to a parachute falls more slowly because of the air resistance between the surface of the parachute and the surrounding air. This slows the descent of the parachute. The same thing happens when a paper spinner or a sycamore seed falls to the ground; air resistance slows down the rate at which it falls.

Water

Water is essential for life and all living things depend on being able to access a supply of water. It has many fascinating properties which young children love to explore – how it moves, the effect it has on different materials, what happens when it is cooled down or heated up, how it makes things move and which things will float or sink when placed in water.

Water is a liquid (see Chapter 6) which covers over 70 per cent of the surface of the planet and is essential to life on earth. Some living things live entirely in the water and all animals and plants are dependent on it for their survival (see Chapters 3, 4 and 5). Water is made up of two chemicals, hydrogen and oxygen, and can exist as either a gas (water vapour or steam), a liquid (water), or a solid (ice) (see Chapter 6).

How water behaves

Water always flows downwards from a high point to the lowest available point. As it does so it spreads out across a surface. Materials such as tissue paper and cotton wool, have the ability to take up water. We call these absorbent materials. Other materials, such as plastic, rubber and metal, can resist water and are non-absorbent. If water is dropped onto a non-absorbent surface it will form small droplets. The droplets have a rounded shape because the water molecules at the outer surface of the drop bind closely to one another to create a 'skin' over the surface. This is called surface tension. Insects such as pond skaters make use of surface tension to walk across the surface of a pond without falling in.

Water cycle

Water is constantly being recycled from the oceans to the atmosphere and back to the oceans again through the processes of evaporation and condensation (see Chapter 6). This is called the water cycle. Water evaporates from the surface of the ocean and moves up into the atmosphere as water vapour. Here it forms clouds containing a mixture of water vapour and ice crystals. Clouds are blown over the land by the wind and some of the water condenses and falls as rain, hail or snow. When rain hits the ground it flows through the soil and eventually finds its way into lakes and rivers. These rivers flow downhill until they reach the sea, returning the water to the ocean again. Along the way the water may be used by plants, drunk by animals or utilised in industrial processes, but it will all eventually find its way back to the sea.

Moving water

Moving water is a source of energy. We can see this when we watch a log floating down a stream or see waves crashing onto a beach. The energy of moving water can be harnessed and used to do work in an old-fashioned watermill or to generate electricity in a hydroelectric power station or tidal barrage (see Chapter 10).

The brakes on a car make use of hydraulics. Pressing on the brake pedal transfers a force to the liquid inside the brake pipes. This force is transmitted by the liquid to the brake pads on the wheel which push against the wheel, increase the friction and slow the car down (see Chapter 7).

Floating and sinking

Objects float in water when there is a balance between the downward pressure of the object on the water and the upward thrust of the water on the object.

In a water tray there are forces acting in all directions. There is a downward pressure through the effect of gravity, a sideways pressure on the sides of the water tray and an upwards pressure pushing towards the surface. This upward pressure is called upthrust.

To experience upthrust try empting a plastic bottle, screwing the lid back on tightly and then holding it under water. The force you need to apply to hold the bottle down is equal to the upthrust of the water pushing the bottle upwards.

When a toy boat is placed in the water tray it takes up space – just as it does in the air. To create this space the boat displaces a volume of water. The volume of water displaced by the boat is equal to the volume of the boat below the surface of the water. The lower down in the water the boat sits the more water it displaces.

When the boat is floating in water the upthrust acting on the boat is equal to the weight of the volume of water displaced. The boat floats because the forces acting on it are balanced.

If you now add cargo to the boat its weight will increase and it will float lower down in the water because it is heavier. The volume of water displaced by the boat will increase so the force of the upthrust increases to balance it. If you add even more weight to the boat there will come a point where the total weight of the boat is greater than the upthrust from the water and the boat will sink to the bottom of the water tray.

Changing the shape of an object will affect whether it will float or sink. A ball of plasticine placed in a bowl of water will sink, but if the same ball of plasticine is flattened and squeezed out into a boat shape and then placed gently on the water it will float. This is because the volume of the plasticine boat is greater than the plasticine ball so it displaces a greater volume of water. You can see the same thing happening in the swimming pool – if you curl up into a ball you sink and if you spread your arms and legs out you float. This is the reason why a lump of iron will sink to the bottom of the sea, but the same iron shaped into the hull of a boat will float on the surface of the sea.

Contexts for learning about air and water

Babies

Providing opportunities for babies to experience moving air and to play with water will stimulate their **curiosity** and **awareness of the world** around them. They will be **using their senses, making choices, expressing preferences** and beginning to **master a range of physical skills**.

≫ Blow, blow, blow

Draw a baby's attention to moving air by blowing gently on an arm or a leg. Talk to the baby as you are doing this:

- Can you feel that?
- Do you like it?

If the baby is enjoying the experience, try blowing harder. Encourage the baby to try blowing too.

Use a hand-held fan to create a gentle waft of air. Try fanning some small scraps of paper to make them dance around. Encourage the babies to chase the paper and to try and catch it.

Look out of the window together on a windy day. Draw attention to the leaves moving on the trees, the clouds moving across the sky. Talk to the baby about what you can see.

Older babies will enjoy using an empty washing-up liquid bottle as an 'air blower'. Encourage them to explore different ways to squeeze the bottle to puff the air out – by using hands or feet, sitting or lying on it.

Observe:

- How individual babies react to these experiences – how they **express preferences** and **communicate their feelings**.
- How they **manipulate** the resources.

Snapshot

Out in the garden Max's key person blows a stream of bubbles above his head. Max watches the bubbles float away in the gentle breeze. As the key person repeats the process Max starts crawling off in the direction the bubbles have gone.

Max is experiencing how moving air can lift very light objects and move them in a particular direction.

≫ Splish, splash

Provide a washing up bowl half full of water and a small selection of spoons, scoops and beakers. Encourage the babies to scoop the water up and pour it out again. Talk to the babies about what they are doing.

Can you scoop up the water?   How full is your beaker?
Can you empty it out again?   Can you lift it?
Does it feel very heavy?   Does it make a big splash?

Put a small colander or a sieve into the water bowl and encourage the babies to explore what happens when water is poured into it. Talk about what is happening.

Put some small pieces of sponge in the bowl and encourage the babies to investigate them. Talk about squeezing and squashing, heavy and light, wet and dry.

Observe:

- How **confident** different babies are in **exploring** the resources.
- How they **manipulate** the different resources.
- The way they **communicate their feelings** about their experiences.
- How **curious** they are and how long they **concentrate**.

Toddlers

≫ Blowing in the wind

Read the story *The Wind Blew* by Pat Hutchins. Talk about all the different items of clothing which were blown away by the wind and jumbled up together.

Look out of the window on a breezy day and look at the movement of the trees and bushes. Talk to the children about the clothes they will need to put on to go outside.

- How can we stop our hats blowing off?
- What do you think will happen to my scarf?

Once outside, encourage the children to fully experience the wind. Run backwards and forwards – into the wind and with the wind behind you.

- Which way is it easiest to move?

Help the children to open their coats out like cloaks to catch as much of the moving air as possible.

- Can you feel the air pushing you along?

Observe:

- **How much attention** different children pay to what they can see outside the window.
- Any words or phrases they use to **describe what they can see.**
- **How confident they are** in moving around outdoors.
- How they **make associations** between the story and their own experiences.

>> Exploring water outdoors

Transferring water from one container to another is an excellent way for young children to develop their **manipulative skills**. Many children will **persist** with this process for **long periods of time** until they have fully mastered the skills involved. During this process children will be learning about how water behaves and discovering **cause and effect**.

On a sunny day, help the children to create a shallow puddle of water. Revisit the puddle at different times during the day and draw the children's attention to how the shape of the puddle has changed.

- What has happened to the puddle?
- Where do you think the water could have gone?

Set up a length of guttering to pour water down.

- What happens to the water when it is poured into the top of the guttering?

Try changing the slope of the guttering.

- What happens to the water now?
- Can you make the water move a boat down the guttering?

Observe:

- How **persistent** different children are as they pour water from one container to another.
- The **manipulative skills** they use.
- The **ideas they put forward** about why the puddle has dried up.
- How the children **explore** the different things they can do with the guttering and the water.
- How well they **cooperate** with one another.

Snapshot

While playing in the water tray Aneesa finds that the front of her trousers have got very wet, despite wearing an apron.

She is discovering the properties of materials – which materials are waterproof and which absorb water and how droplets of water behave on a waterproof surface.

Preschool children

Exploring how air behaves encourages children to **observe closely, think deeply, start to associate cause and effect**, and to **suggest hypotheses** to explain what they can see happening. Investigating air and how it behaves will increase children's **awareness of the world** around them. As air is something we cannot see, but can feel, this is a good opportunity to develop children's experience of **how we use our different senses**.

Preschool children will already have a great deal of experience of how water behaves through their free play exploration. This is an opportunity to look more closely at how things can be made to float or sink. They will be **posing questions, proposing solutions, testing ideas** and **talking about** what they have discovered.

>> **Pneumatic toys**

What you need:

Each pair of children will need

- Two 10ml plastic syringes.
- A short length of plastic tubing which will fit tightly onto the syringes.

What to do:

Look closely at the plastic syringes with the children.

- What happens when you pull the plunger back and then push it in again?
- Can you feel the jet of air?

Show the children how to attach the plastic tubing to the end of the syringe. Squeeze the plunger on the syringe and investigate what happens.

- Where is the jet of air coming from now?
- Could you make something move with this jet of air?

For the next investigation children need to work together in pairs. Help the children to complete the pneumatic mechanism by attaching the other syringe to the tubing. Do this in stages.

1. Push the plunger down on the syringe that is already attached.
2. Pull out the plunger completely on the second syringe.
3. Attach the second syringe to the open end of the tubing.
4. Fit the plunger in and squeeze it gently downwards.

What happens to the plunger on the syringe on the other end?

Observe:

- How individual children **manipulate** the syringes.
- How well they **cooperate** with one another.
- How well they **follow instructions**.
- Their ideas about **what is happening** to the air in the tubing.
- Any connections they make between **cause and effect**.

Talk with the children about how the pneumatic mechanism could be used. This could be a starting point for further exploration leading to a design-and-make project involving pop-up toys or tipper trucks.

>> **'Who sank the boat?'**

What you need:

- A copy of the book *Who Sank the Boat?* by Pamela Allen.
- A water tray or paddling pool.
- Small food containers to use as boats.
- Small world play animals and people.

What to do:

Read the story *Who Sank the Boat* and encourage the children to look carefully at the pictures to see what is happening. Draw attention to where the animals sit in the boat to try to balance their weight.

- What happened to the boat when the cow got in? Why?
- Can you find pictures where the boat is balanced?

Read the story again and focus on observing what is happening to the boat in the water.

- Who did sink the boat?
- Why do you think this happened?

Encourage the children to explore what happens in the story using small world play toys and boats in the water tray.

- How many toys can you fit in the boat before it starts to sink?
- What happens if the passengers all sit on one side of the boat?

Observe:

- Children's **ideas** about what is happening in the boat.
- The **suggestions they make** about 'who did sink the boat'.
- Their **reasoning** behind these conclusions.
- How they **manipulate** the resources.
- How **persistent** they are in following through their investigations.
- How carefully they **observe** what is happening when they load the animals into the boat.

The children could invent 'floating, sinking and sunk' stories of their own using other characters such as pirates and dinosaurs. The stories *Mr Archimedes' Bath* and *Mr Gumpy's Outing* are good starting points for exploring displacement and floating.

Developing effective scientific communication

When children are exploring air and water there will be many opportunities for conversations and discussions. These are the ideal times to introduce scientific terminology and model how it should be used. Having this vocabulary to draw on will help children to express their ideas and explain their observations accurately.

air	wind	blow	jet
push	pull	force	pneumatic
syringe	plunger	tubing	light
heavy	spin	streamer	windmill
float	sinking	sunk	balance
wet	dry	splash	damp
big	small	shape	heavy
light	weight	water	bottom
surface	boat	side	passengers

To prompt children to carry on their explorations of air and water, and to develop their scientific thinking and reasoning skills, you could pose the following challenges:

- Can you find a way to lift up a wooden brick without touching it?
- Can you use air to make a toy car move?
- Is air strong enough to knock down a wall of bricks?
- Does plasticene float or sink?
- Can you find a way to make water turn a wheel?
- Can you make water flow uphill?

Equipment and resources

Children under 3

Lightweight fabric and scarves
Streamers and ribbon sticks
Windmills
Wind chimes
Bubble mixture and bubble blowers
Large plastic discovery trays
Plastic jugs and beakers
Transparent plastic buckets
Water tray

Drainpipes and guttering
Plastic bowls, spoons, scoops, cups and beakers
Plastic sieve
Colander
Plastic funnels
First Explorer's Water pump (*Reflections on Learning: www.reflectionsonlearning.co.uk*)
Stories and rhymes about water and air

3 to 5 year olds

Streamers and ribbon sticks
Windmills
Wind chimes
Bubble mixture and bubble blowers
Plastic syringes
Plastic tubing
Pipettes
Funnels
Large plastic discovery trays
Plastic jugs and beakers
Transparent plastic buckets
Water tray
Drainpipes and guttering
Hosepipe and source of running water
Plastic bowls, spoons, scoops, cups and beakers
Plastic sieves
Colander
Small wooden or plastic boats
Let's Explore Air and Water (*Reflections on Learning: www.reflectionsonlearning.co.uk*)
The Wind Blew (Pat Hutchins: Aladdin Books)
Who Sank the Boat? (Pamela Allen: Puffin Books)
Mr Archimedes' Bath (Pamela Allen: Puffin Books)
Mr Gumpy's Outing (John Burningham: Red Fox)

Further reading

Chalufour, I. and Worth, K. (2005) *Exploring Water with Young Children*. St. Paul, MN: Redleaf.
Moomaw, S. and Hieronmymus, B. (1997) *More than Magnets*. St. Paul, MN: Redleaf.
Smith, B. (2004) *The Science You Need to Know*. Hatfield: Association for Science Education.

9 Magnets and Magnetism

Chapter Summary

This chapter looks at the phenomenon of magnetism and how we experience it in our daily lives. It describes how magnets are made and the properties of different magnets and looks at the way in which the Earth acts as a giant magnet. Understanding how magnets behave provides the context for giving opportunities to children to explore magnetism safely and to enjoy the experience of being able to make things move without touching them.

Background knowledge

Uses of magnetism

Magnets and magnetism have an enormous effect on our lives as we make use of magnetic forces in so many different ways. Magnets are used in every home, as catches on cupboard doors and in the rubber-coated magnetic strip which holds the freezer door shut. Magnetic clasps can often be found on handbags, purses or necklaces and fridge magnets are used to attach notes and photographs to metal surfaces.

In the electronics industry a magnetic film is used to record data on swipe cards, video and audio tapes, to store information on computer disk drives and magnets are used in loudspeakers and microphones. Large magnets are used to sort cans in recycling centres and to move crushed vehicles around in scrap yards. Perhaps the most important use we make of magnetism in modern life is in the generation of electrical energy in power stations (see Chapter 10).

What is magnetism?

Nobody can answer this question fully – scientists have a number of theories to explain the phenomenon of magnetism but none of these can completely explain what magnetism is. It is easier to describe what magnets do rather than to say what magnetism is.

Magnetism has been known about for at least two thousand years when the properties of one type of naturally occurring iron ore, called lodestone, were discovered. A piece of lodestone suspended on a length of string will turn to point in a north–south direction, and was used as an early form of compass. Later discoveries found that magnetism is a particular property of some metals. The most common of these are iron, cobalt and nickel, and combinations of metals (alloys) such as steel.

How is a magnet made?

To understand how a magnet works it is useful to think about how the millions of tiny particles which make up the metal are arranged. In a non-magnetic material these particles are randomly arranged. In a magnet the particles are arranged in a regular way with one end pointing north and the other end pointing south.

One end of the magnet becomes its north pole and the other end its south pole. The more ordered this arrangement the stronger the magnet will be.

A new magnet can be created by bringing a piece of magnetic metal, such as iron, into contact with an existing magnet. Inside the piece of metal the millions of tiny particles will be all jumbled up and facing in different directions. When the magnet is placed next to the piece of metal the particles will begin to line up to face in a north–south direction and the piece of metal itself will become a magnet. Repeating this process by stroking the piece of metal with the magnet – always moving in the same direction – will increase the magnetism in the metal. This is why a string of paperclips will hang from the end of a magnet. The stronger the magnet, the greater the force of magnetism, the longer the string of paperclips will be.

The Earth as a magnet

The reason a compass needle turns to point in a north–south direction is because the Earth behaves as if it is a giant magnet, with a North and a South Pole. This is thought to be due to the geological structure of the planet and the presence of a molten metallic core at the Earth's centre. The magnetic North and South Poles are near, but not in exactly the same place as the geographical North and South Poles. Around the Earth, like every other magnet, there is an invisible force of magnetism called a force field. Inside a compass the magnetic pointer is free to turn in any direction. When it interacts with the Earth's force field the pointer always turns to point north.

Using magnets

Every magnet has a north and a south pole. You will find that 'like poles' (north/north or south/south) repel, or move away from one another when brought together. 'Unlike poles' (north/south) will attract one another and move towards one another.

When a magnet is brought close to a magnetic material, such as a metal paper clip, the metal will be attracted to the magnet and will jump towards the end of the magnet. Materials which are non-magnetic, such as wood or paper, will not be affected by the magnet and so will not move.

Magnetic forces can be felt through non-magnetic materials. If a range of magnetic objects is placed on a plastic or wooden tray and a magnet is moved around underneath the tray, the objects on the tray can be moved around – by an apparently invisible force.

Magnets come in different shapes and sizes and can sometimes appear to be made of very different materials:

- *Bar magnets*
  These have a north and south pole at opposite ends and are often colour coded blue and red. Sometimes the metal bar is encased in plastic which can make it difficult for children to see that it is the metal and not the plastic which is the magnetic material. Bar magnets should be stored alongside one another in pairs with opposite ends next to each other.
- *Horseshoe magnets*
  These consist of a north and south pole at either end of the horseshoe. Giant horseshoe magnets often have a north and a south facing magnet at either end separated by a large plastic hoop. The magnets are best stored with a short metal bar – a 'keeper' – spanning the two poles.
- *Ring magnets*
  These circular magnets have the north and south poles on opposite surfaces of the ring and a hole in the centre. They should be stored in pairs with opposite poles facing one another. If two ring magnets are threaded onto a short wooden or plastic rod with their like poles facing one another, a very interesting effect is seen. The two ring magnets will repel one another so the upper magnet appears to float in space.

- *Magnetic marbles*
  These consist of a hollow plastic marbles with small bar magnets inside. The marbles will stick to one another as the bar magnets inside them line up with opposite poles facing one another. The stronger the magnets inside the marbles, the longer the string of marbles will be.
- *Magnetic strip or sheet*
  These magnets are not very powerful but have the advantage of being flexible. It is not the rubber or plastic itself which is acting as a magnet. Instead it has small amounts of magnetic material incorporated into it when it is being manufactured.

All magnets will lose their magnetism if they are dropped or heated up, or if the like poles are forced together regularly. All these actions disrupt the arrangement of the particles in the magnet. Store and use magnets carefully and do not allow them anywhere near electrical equipment, including computers, video tapes, DVD players and televisions.

Contexts for learning about magnetism

Safety first

Magnets could be harmful if swallowed so toys containing small magnetic parts are not suitable for unsupervised use by babies or toddlers. The effects of magnetism can still be explored by children under 3 in carefully supervised situations by using large magnets which are too big to cause a swallowing hazard.

Exploring around the setting using a magnet could present a danger to computer equipment, tape recorders and music players. When working with toddlers ensure any electronic components have been safely stored away before bringing magnets out. Talk to preschool children about what equipment to avoid when exploring sensibly with magnets and supervise their activities closely.

Babies

Exploring how materials behave when they come into contact with a magnet will prompt babies' **curiosity**. They will be developing their **problem-solving skills** and learning how to **manipulate materials and resources**.

Always supervise babies very carefully when playing with magnets and make sure these are stored out of reach when not being used.

>> **The power of attraction**

Babies can experience the effects of magnetism by using a large horseshoe magnet and a metal tray. Under careful supervision help the children to explore the way the magnet and tray move towards one another when they are brought close together. Let a baby try to push the magnet over the surface of the tray and to pull the two objects apart.

Observe:

- How **interested** the baby is in the activity.
- **How long the baby persists** with the exploration.
- **How often** the baby wants to repeat the experience.
- What other materials the baby tries to **explore** with the magnet.
- How the baby **manipulates** the magnet.

When talking to the baby during this activity use the words, 'pull', 'push', 'metal' and 'attract' to describe what is happening.

>> **Magnets all around**

Draw the babies' attention to any appropriate examples of magnetism being used around the setting. For example, the magnetic rubber strip for door closures, magnetic picture boards, and soft toys which cling on to things through magnets concealed in their feet and hands. Use your judgement and avoid anything where children's fingers could be trapped or magnets could be picked up and swallowed.

Observe:

- The way in which the babies **explore** the effects of magnetism.
- How they **apply knowledge** gained in one context to a different situation.

Snapshot

Zac picks up a giant horseshoe magnet and waves it round in front of him. When the metal bowl becomes attached to the magnet he sits up in surprise. First he shakes the magnet to try to dislodge the bowl and then starts pulling at it. Zac's key person helps him to prise the magnet off the bowl and Zac immediately repeats his exploration.

Zac is making his first discoveries about magnetic forces.

Toddlers

In exploring the effects of magnetism toddlers will be **trying out ideas**, **solving problems** and **overcoming challenges**. They will be developing their **manipulative skills** and will have opportunities to demonstrate **persistence** and **resilience**.

Supervise toddlers closely when playing with magnets and make sure all magnets are stored out of reach when not being used.

>> ### Magnetic building blocks

Plastic building blocks which have magnets sealed inside them are interesting resources to use. The magnets affect the properties of the blocks and how they behave, enabling toddlers to build interesting and unusual structures.

Observe:

- How **interested** individual children are in the blocks and how they behave.
- The way they **experiment** with the blocks to **find out** how they behave in different situations.
- How they **use this information** to manipulate the blocks to create the effects they want.
- The way in which they **cope with the challenges** of building with materials which behave in an unusual way.

>> ### Magnetic train sets

Some simple train sets have magnets at either end of the engine and carriages so they can be linked together by magnetic attraction. By exploring the ways in which the parts can be joined together toddlers will be discovering for themselves one of the basic principles of magnetism – unlike poles attract one another and like poles repel one another.

Observe:

- The way the children **handle the train parts** and **explore** how they fit together.
- How they **learn from experience**.
- Any **comments** and ideas they suggest about how the parts of the train behave.

Snapshot

Amy is playing with the trucks from the magnetic train set on the wooden floor. As she moves one of the trucks towards the stationary truck on the floor she notices that is spins round before the two trucks join together. Her shout of excitement alerts her friend Grace to the fact that something exciting is happening and she comes over to join her.

The two children now move the trucks backwards and forwards across the floor looking at ways to repeat Amy's discovery. They continue to play with the trucks for another 20 minutes, moving them backwards and forwards and from side to side.

Amy's key person observes what is happening and takes a series of photographs, but she does not interrupt the children's exploration. Later in the day she shares the photographs with the children and they talk again about what they saw happening.

Amy and Grace are learning through first-hand experience that the like poles of a magnet repel one another and unlike poles attract and that the force of magnetism can act over a distance.

Preschool children

As children build their experience of the effects of magnetism there are opportunities for them to begin to **explore** the magnetic properties of different materials in a **systematic way**. This involves **planning and predicting, observing and hypothesizing, investigating and sharing ideas, reflecting and reporting**.

≫ What will a magnet attract?

What you need:

- A selection of bar or horseshoe magnets.
- A selection of objects made of different materials including metal, wood, cardboard, plastic and rubber.
- Access to different areas in your setting, both indoors and out.

What to do:

Working with a small group of children, allow time for them to investigate what happens when the magnets come into contact with the different objects.

Encourage them to sort and classify the objects by exploring:

- Which objects are attracted to the magnet?
- Which objects are not attracted to a magnet?

Help the children to sort the objects into two groups:

- Things that are attracted to a magnet.
- Things that are not attracted to a magnet.

Encourage the children to look closely at the objects in the two groups. Discuss what materials the objects in each of the groups are made of.

- Were there any surprises?

(1p coins are interesting – some will be attracted to a magnet, but not others.)

Now go on a 'magnet safari' around your setting, indoors and out.

Remind the children to keep the magnets away from computers, TVs and other electrical equipment.

Each child will need a magnet. Walk around the setting and give the children the opportunity to discover which everyday objects are magnetic. Use the outdoor environment to investigate brickwork, tree trunks, drain covers, drainpipe fixings, plant pots and garden tools.

Make a list of all the things which a magnet is attracted to. This is a good opportunity to talk to children about the importance of recording observations.

Observe:

- The way in which children **sort and classify** the objects.
- How **curious** they are about exploring the environment using magnets.
- How they **describe the discoveries** they have made.
- Any **predictions** they make about which things a magnet will be attracted to.
- Any **evidence they present** to support these predictions.

Snapshot

At the start of the morning session the children are discussing what they are going to do that day. Connor, who for several days has spent a lot of time playing with a magnetic shape puzzle, announces that he is going to be a 'magnet master'. His plan is to find some more magnetic materials around the setting which he can add to his puzzle.

The group discuss what a 'magnet master' might do and where in the setting he might go. Having chosen two magnets from the Exploration and Investigation drawer, Connor goes around the setting testing materials to see what his magnets will be attracted to. At the end of the morning session he shows the rest of the group the new magnetic puzzle he has made, with paperclips, coins, metal tags and keys added to it.

Connor is learning about the properties of materials and that some types of metal are attracted to magnets.

>> The best magnet in the world

Agreeing what the word 'best' means is a good opportunity for **negotiation and discussion** and helps children to **express and clarify their ideas**. What you need:

- A wooden or plastic tray.
- A variety of magnetic objects – large paper clips, magnetic marbles or counters, spoons, scissors, coins.
- A selection of magnets of different shapes and sizes – bar magnets, ring magnets, magnetic wands and horseshoe magnets.

What to do:

In this activity focus on the children deciding which magnet they think is the best, and giving reasons for their choices. Explain to the children that you are trying to find 'the best magnet in the world' and you need their help.

Place the tray of magnetic objects in an area of the room where it can be accessed by pairs of children working together. Give each pair of children the time to investigate the magnets and to answer these two questions:

- Which magnet is the best?
- Why is it the best?

Think about how you will record the children's answers to these questions and the thinking behind their opinions.

As a group help the children to share their ideas and opinions on which is the best magnet.

- Does everybody agree?
- Why do you think your choice is the best?
- Do you like anybody else's ideas?

Discuss what is meant by 'best' – the biggest, the one that picks up the most objects, the one that picks up the biggest object, or the most attractive one!

Observe:

- How individual children **organize information.**
- How they **express their ideas**.
- How they **use evidence** to support their ideas.

Developing effective scientific communication

Exploring the effects of magnetism is always an exciting thing to do. Children will be fascinated by the way in which some things can be made to move 'as if by magic', so exploring magnetism presents an ideal opportunity to encourage speaking and listening skills. Investigating what magnets can do is also a good opportunity to develop children's close observation skills as they describe the way different materials behave under the influence of a magnet. By using the correct scientific terminology in discussion with the children you will be helping them to acquire the vocabulary they need to describe this fascinating phenomenon.

magnet	magnetic	north	metal
bar	pull	south	paper
ring	push	pole	plastic
horseshoe	stick	attract	wood
marble	compass	repel	pottery

Challenge children's scientific thinking and problem-solving skills by inviting them to investigate questions such as:

- Are all metals magnetic?
- What happens when two magnets are brought close to one another?
- Can you make things move by using a magnet?
- How many sheets of paper can the force of a magnet be felt through?
- Can you built a taller tower with magnetic blocks or wooden blocks?
- How many carriages can a magnetic train pull?

Equipment and resources

Children under 3

Large horseshoe magnet
First Explorers Giant Horseshoe magnet (*Reflections on Learning: www. reflectionsonlearning.co.uk*)
Collection of metal spoons and bowls
Jumbo Mag set (*Reflections on Learning: www.reflectionsonlearning.co.uk*)
Brio magnetic train sets

3 to 5 year olds

Giant horseshoe magnet
Plastic-cased bar magnets
Ring magnets
Magnetic push-pull cars
Magnetic fishing game
Let's Explore Magnetism kit (*Reflections on Learning: www.reflectionsonlearning.co.uk*)
Magformers construction set (*Reflections on Learning: www.reflectionsonlearning.co.uk*)
Magnetic wands, chips and marbles
Magneblocks (*Reflections on Learning: www.reflectionsonlearning.co.uk*)
Brio magnetic train sets
Collection of magnetic and non-magnetic metals

Further reading

Ashbrook, P. (2003) *Science is Simple*. Beltsville, MD: Gryphon House.
Farrow, S. (1999) *The Really Useful Science Book*. London: Falmer.
Sherwood, E.A., Williams, R.A. and Rockwell, R.E. (1990) *More Mudpies to Magnets: Science for Young Children*. Beltsville, MD: Gryphon House.

10 Electricity

Chapter Summary

This chapter looks at how we use electricity, describes how an electrical current is generated and at what the difference is between mains electricity and batteries. It also looks at the properties of the components used to create a simple electrical circuit and at how a torch works.

This creates a context for providing opportunities for babies and toddlers to appreciate the influence which electricity has on their lives and for older preschool children to explore simple electrical circuits.

Background knowledge

Uses of electricity

Electricity is a form of energy which is very useful to us in the modern world. We have come to rely on it in our everyday lives and young children will be familiar with what electricity helps us to do – to see in the dark, watch television, enjoy music and computer games, cook, wash clothes and mow the lawn. Electricity is very convenient as it can be stored, moved through cables and wires and turned on and off at the flick of a switch. It can also be easily converted into other forms of energy, including light energy in light bulbs, heat energy in electric fires or cookers and sound energy in radios and music systems.

Electrical current

The term 'electricity' comes from the word 'electron'. Electrons are part of the structure of the atoms that everything in the world is made up of (see Chapter 6). All atoms consist of a nucleus in the centre which has a positive charge and one or more outer shells of electrons, each of which has a negative charge. In its stable state the total amount of positive charge in the nucleus of the atom is balanced by the number of negatively charged electrons in the outer shells. In certain types of materials – those which are conductors of electricity – the electrons circulating around the nucleus can be displaced by heat or by chemical reaction. It is the movement of these negatively charged electrons which creates an electric current.

Mains electricity

Mains electricity is generated in power stations using a source of energy such as coal, gas, oil, nuclear fuel or water power. In a power station fuel is burned to heat water and create steam. The steam turns a generator in which large magnets spin round inside a huge wire coil. This creates a current of electricity. Renewable energy systems, such as hydroelectric power stations and wind farms, use the power of falling water or wind to turn the generator directly, without the need to burn fuel.

The electrical current generated in a power station is transported across the country at high voltage to provide the power we use in our homes, schools, offices, shops and factories. When it enters our homes, settings and schools mains electricity is at 240 volts. This is in contrast to the voltage of a battery which will be in the range of 1.5 volts to 5 volts. Mains electricity is therefore extremely dangerous. It is essential that children, from a very early age, understand that electrical sockets are potentially dangerous and should not be touched.

Conductors and insulators

Electricity passes through some materials more easily than others. Materials which allow electricity to pass through are called conductors. The best conductors of electricity are gold, copper, aluminium and steel. These metals are good conductors of electricity because the electrons in the outer shells of the atoms they are made up of are not closely attracted to the nucleus and are therefore free to move when an electric circuit is created.

Materials which do not conduct electricity are called insulators. Plastic, rubber and ceramic are all good insulators. In these materials the electrons are closely bound to the central nucleus and are therefore not free to move. Insulators play a very important role in protecting us from the danger of receiving an electric shock. Electrical wire is covered in plastic or rubber, plugs and sockets are made of plastic, and ceramic separators are used to keep high voltage electric cables isolated from one another.

Batteries

A battery is made of two or more cells and is a source of electricity which it is safe to handle and to use. A battery is a convenient way to store small amounts of electrical energy. It is made up of an insulating material on the outside, two metal terminals or connecting points and a central core containing chemicals. These chemicals react with one another to create a build-up of electrons at one terminal of the battery, giving it a negative charge. The other terminal of the battery has a deficit of electrons and has a positive charge.

When the two terminals of the battery are connected to one another by a material which conducts electricity, the electrons transfer from one atom to another throughout the circuit. This creates a current of electricity from the negative terminal of the battery to the positive terminal. This is an electrical circuit. Eventually the chemicals in the battery are used up and no more electrons are released. The battery is then flat and is no longer a source of energy.

Electrical circuits

When a circuit is made the electrical energy will be conducted from the battery through a loop of wire and metal components and back to the battery again. The electricity is conducted in one direction, from the negative terminal of the battery to the positive terminal through the metal components in the circuit. The wires in the circuit are usually covered in plastic to insulate them and make them safe to handle. This can sometimes cause confusion as children may think that the wires themselves are made of plastic. Spend time looking closely at the different parts of a circuit so you can see how all the metal parts join together in order for the electricity to be conducted. Bulbs are usually screwed into plastic bulb holders when they are introduced into circuits. Again, careful examination will show that it is the metal connections in the bulb holder that the electricity is conducted through, not the plastic.

How a bulb works

In order to see the effect of electrical energy in the circuit we need to introduce something into the circuit which is powered by electricity, for example, a torch bulb, a buzzer or a small motor. When a torch bulb is included in a circuit the electric current makes a detour through the metal parts of the bulb. The bottom part of the bulb is made of metal and has two terminals on it, one on the bottom and one on the side. If you look closely at the glass-covered part of the bulb it is possible to see a very fine piece of coiled wire called the filament. This piece of wire, made of a metal called tungsten, joins the two terminals of the bulb to one another. The flow of electricity has to go through the tungsten wire to get from one terminal of the bulb to the other. Because the wire is very thin it is difficult for the electricity to pass through it so a large amount of heat energy is created. The filament starts to glow and give off both heat energy and light energy. If the filament was exposed to oxygen in the air it would burn, so instead the bulb is filled with a gas called argon to prevent burning.

Adding bulbs to a circuit

The more electrical energy the battery supplies the brighter the bulb will glow. Adding another battery to the circuit will provide more electrical energy but it is possible to overload the system and cause the filament to overheat and the bulb to 'blow'. If you look very carefully at a blown bulb it is often possible to see the broken filament dangling inside the globe of the bulb.

Adding a second bulb into the circuit alongside the first will affect the brightness of the two bulbs. Both bulbs will glow with equal brightness but they will not be as bright as one bulb on its own. If one of the bulbs in the circuit is unscrewed, or goes out, the other bulb will also go out, because the circuit has been broken. This arrangement of two bulbs in a circuit next to one another is called 'bulbs in series'.

It is possible to have two bulbs in a circuit which work independently. To do this each bulb needs to be connected to the battery by its own set of wires. This arrangement is called 'bulbs in parallel'. In this arrangement both bulbs will glow brightly and unscrewing one bulb will not affect the other bulb as it has its own connections to the battery.

Switches

A switch is something which can stop the conduction of electricity in a circuit. A switch is made of a conducting material, and when it is in the 'on' position the electricity can pass through it and complete the circuit. When it is in the 'off' position there is a break in the circuit so no electricity can be conducted.

Switches in toys, torches, lights and electrical goods are always covered by insulating material to protect us from harm so the mechanism of the switch is hidden.

Buzzers and motors

Buzzers and small electric motors can be used in simple circuits. If a buzzer is added to a circuit the electricity is conducted through the buzzer mechanism, causing the metal parts of the buzzer to vibrate. The air inside the buzzer then vibrates creating sound waves which travel to our ears so we hear a noise (see Chapter 11).

Electric motors are designed to convert electrical energy into movement energy. The electrical energy from the battery creates a small magnetic field which causes the metal parts of the motor to rotate and the drive shaft to spin round (see Chapter 9).

Torches

A torch is a simple example of a machine that is powered by electricity. All torches are constructed slightly differently but all have the same basic layout. The power source for the torch is the batteries which fit into the body of the torch: the bulb is located at the end and the switch mechanism is usually found on the side. For the torch to work the batteries have to be put in the right way round so the positive terminal of one battery is in contact with the negative terminal of the other battery in order to complete the circuit.

Because of the location of the components and the arrangement of the insulating materials in a torch it is not easy to see the connections between different parts of the electrical circuit. In particular it is often hard to see how the connection is made from the metal spring at the end of the battery compartment and the bulb. For this reason dismantling a torch with young children is not a good way to help them see what an electric circuit looks like.

Contexts for learning about electricity

Safety note

- Make sure that you have talked to the children about the difference between mains electricity and batteries.
- Ensure that the children understand that whilst the equipment you have given them is safe to investigate, plugs, sockets, switches and electric lamps are not.
- Have all electrical equipment in your setting checked annually by a qualified electrician to ensure its safety.
- If using electrical appliances outside use a heavy duty outdoor extension cable with a circuit breaker incorporated into it.

- Protect unused sockets with safety covers.
- Position electrical equipment as close as possible to sockets and tape down any trailing leads.
- Batteries should never be put in the mouth.
- Batteries must never be dismantled as they contain strong chemicals which can cause burns to the skin.
- Occasionally batteries will start to corrode and leak if they have been left for a long time in a damp place. Dispose of these carefully.
- Old batteries should always be disposed of through a battery recycling facility to prevent their chemicals contaminating household rubbish.

Babies

Battery-operated toys are a part of modern day society, so from a very young age babies are able to experience the effects which the use of electricity can have on their lives. While **using their senses** to explore sound and movement, they will be **expressing preferences** and gaining an element of **control over their surroundings**.

〉〉 Toys which move

Battery-operated mobiles which turn and play a tune are a source of fascination for very young babies. By talking to a baby about 'switching the mobile on' and 'looking to see what happens' you will begin to build an understanding of **cause and effect**.

Observe:

- How the baby **responds** to the movement of the mobile – through body movement, facial expression, using the eyes to track movement, making sounds.
- As the baby becomes more familiar which the mobile, pause before switching it on and note the way he or she begins to **predict** what will happen – through looking, moving or vocalising.

〉〉 Baby gym

Some designs of baby gym include battery-operated components which a baby can learn to activate for him or herself, often through leaning on a pressure switch.

Observe:

- How a baby **reacts** to the accidental switching on of one of the gym's components – talk about 'switching on' and 'making something happen'.
- How **curious** the baby is about how the different parts of the gym work.
- How quickly a baby learns to **control his or her surroundings** by switching on the components of the gym.

Toddlers

This is an important time for toddlers to **learn sensible rules** about handling electricity safely, without becoming afraid of it. Many toddlers are fascinated by **controlling their environment** by switching items on and off to make things happen. On/off switches on equipment such as tape recorders, overhead projectors and computers are safe to touch and operating them helps to give children **choice and independence**. However, each setting will have its own safety policy setting regarding the operation of electrical equipment.

>> Battery-operated vehicles

Battery-operated cars and trucks can provide an interesting and safe way for toddlers to explore some of the effects of electricity. Pre-programmed toys which always behave in the same way, such as the Tolo First Friends range, are easier for toddlers to manipulate than more complex radio-controlled vehicles.

Talk to toddlers about what happens when the vehicle is switched on.

- How does the toy behave?
- Does it move?
- Does it make a noise?
- Do the lights flash?
- Does it do the same thing every time?
- Where do you think the energy comes from?

Observe:

- How **curious** they are about how the toy works.
- How closely the children **observe** the different movements the vehicle makes and any **comments they make.**

- Any **predictions** they make about how the toy will behave.
- The **fine motor skills** they develop through manipulating the switches.

>> Battery-operated soft toys

There is a wide range of very sophisticated talking, moving toys produced for young children. Exploring what these can do is interesting and amusing, and also provides the opportunity to develop toddlers' observational skills and to introduce some simple scientific language.

Observe:

- Which children are most **interested in** and **curious about** the toy?
- The **skills they use** to explore the toy to find what it can do.
- How they **manipulate** the toy.
- Any **comments** they make about how they think the toy works and whether they think it is 'alive' or not.

Snapshot

Emily is fascinated by the battery-operated car. She switches it on and lets it run across the carpeted floor. She shrieks with laughter when the car flashes its lights and hoots its horn and dashes over to pick it up when it stops. When she takes it out to run over the wooden surface of the corridor she discovers that the car goes further than she had anticipated and knocks into a chair at the end, sending it off course. She repeats the experience twice more with the same result and then decides to move further back down the corridor to give the car a longer track to run on. This time the car stops just before it hits the chair. Emily is delighted.

Emily is discovering that electricity can make things move, about how simple control mechanisms work and about how different materials can affect the movement of the car.

Preschool children

While investigating how to create simple circuits preschool children will be **developing their skills of observation, practising the fine motor skills** needed to manipulate small objects and building their **understanding of**

cause and effect. They will also be **posing questions, discussing ideas** and **seeking solutions**.

Adult support in this process involves **providing the appropriate equipment and resources, carrying out risk assessments** to ensure children's safety and **facilitating exploration through well structured questions**.

Making a simple circuit

When introducing components for making a circuit to older preschool children it is important to keep things very simple and focus on the links between the different components in the circuit. The activity will work best with a small group and needs adult involvement.

What you need:

- Several 3-volt torch bulbs.
- Batten bulb holders to screw the bulbs into.
- Leads with a crocodile clip at each end.
- Flat shaped 4.5-volt batteries – these have the two terminals for the battery at the top and are easy to fix the crocodile clips to.
- Magnifiers.

What to do:

Encourage the children to work individually or in pairs, looking closely at a light bulb through a magnifier. To help them focus on what they are looking at, ask:

- Can you see the thin wire inside the bulb?
- Where does it go?

Provide the children with just a battery and a bulb. Pose this challenge:

- Do you think you could make the torch bulb light up?

Children will need some time to explore this, but eventually someone will be successful and will have discovered just where to hold the bulb against the terminals of the battery to complete a circuit.

This is the best way to demonstrate the connections in a simple circuit.

Now introduce the other electrical components – the bulb holders, the leads and crocodile clips and the batteries. Ask:

- Can you find the metal parts of the bulb, the bulb holder, the leads and the battery?
- Why do you think the ends of the leads are called crocodile clips?

Encourage them to talk about and describe the different electrical components.

Give the children time to investigate for themselves how to use the components to light up the bulb.

When the several children have successfully made a simple circuit ask them to demonstrate to the rest of the group. Pose questions such as:

- Can you describe what you did to make the bulb light up?
- Which things are joined together?
- Can you think of a good way to make the light go off again?

Observe:

- How they **observe** the bulb and the words they use to **describe what they see.**
- The way in which they **describe** the components of the electrical circuit and any **ideas they put forward about how they work.**
- How they **manipulate** the components of the circuit.
- How **persistent** and **interested** they are in their explorations.

The discoveries which children make during this investigation will invariably suggest new ideas and theories to try out.

>> Make a noise

This activity enables children to investigate what happens when other electrical components are added to a circuit.

What you need:

- Flat shaped 4.5-volt battery.
- Leads with crocodile clips at each end.
- Open push switch.
- Buzzer.

What to do:

In one area of your setting, have a tray of electrical components available for the children to investigate. Vary the components which you include. In this instance, make a battery, leads, a switch and a buzzer available. Do not tell the children what the 'new' component is or what it will do.

Wait to see what happens when the children notice that a new component has been added to the selection with which they are familiar.

When you hear the buzzer work, gather the group of children together and talk to them about what has happened. Ask:

- Can you tell me how you made the buzzer work?
- Where else have you heard a buzzer?
- What are they used for?
- Can we have a buzzer and a light bulb in the same circuit?

Observe:

- Which children are most **interested** in **exploring** the electrical components.
- How children **collaborate** with one another.
- How different children **pose problems** for themselves and find **solutions** to these problems.
- What **innovative ideas** they come up with for **creating** new circuits.

Why doesn't it work?

- Check that the batteries are not flat.
- Make sure that the filament in the bulb isn't broken.
- Check that the bulb is screwed in tightly.
- Make sure that all the connections are secure.
- If something doesn't work, try it the other way round – buzzers only work when connected the right way round.

Developing effective scientific communication

During the course of exploring and investigating the effects of electricity adults can introduce children to the correct scientific terminology during conversations, while asking questions and when making comments. Gaining this basic scientific vocabulary will help to build their conceptual understanding and enable them to communicate their ideas more clearly.

start	stop	move	switch
on	off	press	noise
tune	sound	light	flash
bulb	battery	bulb holder	crocodile clip
wire	lead	circuit	buzzer
conductor	insulator		

Children's scientific thinking and practical skills will be developed by posing open-ended questions which can encourage them to explore and investigate. These could include:

- How far do you think the battery-operated car can go?
- Will the car go faster if it is going downhill?
- Could you make a light for the dolls' house?
- Which torch is the best?
- Do all musical mobiles play the same tune?
- What happens when we switch the lights off?

Equipment and resources

Children under 3

Battery-operated mobiles
Tolo: First Friends Construction
Tolo: First Friends Traffic set
Battery-operated soft toys
Large torch

3 to 5 year olds

Tolo: First Friends Construction
Tolo: First Friends Traffic set
Battery-operated soft toys
Torches
Let's Explore Electricity kit (*Reflections on Learning: www.reflectionsonlearning.co.uk*)

Further reading

Brunton, P. and Thornton, L. (2004) *The Little Book of Light and Shadow*. Lutterworth: Featherstone Education.
Farrow, S. (1999) *The Really Useful Science Book*. London: Falmer.
Johnstone, J. (2005) *Early Explorations in Science* (2nd edition). Maidenhead: Open University Press.

Sound

Chapter Summary

This chapter looks at the influence sound has on our daily lives, at how sounds are made and at how we hear sound. It reviews how different musical instruments make sounds and how volume and pitch affect the quality of the sounds we hear.

This creates the context for helping young children to explore sounds and to become more aware of how they can use their sense of hearing to provide them with information about the world around them.

Background knowledge

Sound and hearing

Sound is an important part of our daily lives. The ability to hear and make sounds helps us to gain information about what is going on in our environment as well as to communicate with one another. Sounds are used to warn of danger through alarm bells or car horns, to provide information and entertainment through radio and television broadcasts, to affect our moods and emotions through music and to exchange information and experience through talking and listening.

From a very early age children will be aware of sounds all around them – voices, body sounds, weather, animals, vehicles, machinery, music, television and toys. Exploring sound will heighten children's awareness of how they use their senses, build the auditory discrimination skills essential for successful language development and increase their appreciation of the aesthetics of musical expression.

How sounds are made

All sounds are caused by small repeated movements called vibrations. For example, when we speak our voice boxes vibrate, when an engine is running the metal parts of the engine are vibrating, and when a radio is playing the metal and plastic parts of the speakers are vibrating. In all these examples the vibrations, or small mechanical movements, make the air surrounding them vibrate, or move backwards and forwards. These vibrations, or sound waves, move outwards in all directions from the object making the sound. When these sound waves reach our ears we then hear the sound.

Sound travels very quickly through air – at approximately 330 metres per second – but about 1 million times more slowly than the speed of light. This means that you can see a sound being created a long way off before you can hear it. This explains why jet aircraft have often passed overhead before we hear the sound of the engine and look upwards.

Although sound usually travels through air and makes the molecules of air vibrate in a sound wave, sound can also travel through solid objects and through water. If you put your ear up against a door you can hear clearly what is happening on the other side. If you put your head under water in the bath and then tap on the side of the bath you can hear the sound of the tapping very loudly.

Musical instruments

All musical instruments make sound by vibrating. The various sounds that different instruments make depend on what they are made of, how big they are and how the vibrations are made. For example, a drum makes a sound when the skin of the drum is struck with a drumstick. This makes the surface of the drum vibrate and these vibrations are passed on to the air surrounding the drum. You can see these vibrations if you put a small amount of sand or rice on the surface of a drum and then tap the drum. The sand jumps up and down from the vibrations of the drum skin.

In a stringed instrument such as a guitar the sound is made by plucking the strings to make them vibrate. The air surrounding the string vibrates and sound waves are created. In a wind instrument such as a clarinet blowing through the reed at the top of the instrument makes the reed vibrate and this vibration is passed down the column of air inside the body of the clarinet. Brass instruments such as trumpets and trombones make a sound from the vibration of the lips of the player through the mouthpiece of the instrument.

Volume and pitch

Volume is the term used when talking about how loud or soft a sound is. Loud sounds create big vibrations and soft sounds create smaller vibrations. The distance the sound wave has to travel before it reaches the ear also affects how loud it sounds. Sounds that are made further away appear quieter to us.

Pitch is the term used to describe how high or low a sound is. High-pitched sounds create vibrations which are very close together. These are called high frequency sounds. Low-pitched sounds create slower vibrations which are more spaced out. These are low frequency sounds.

Humans can hear sounds in a frequency range between 20 vibrations per second (very low-pitched sounds) and 18,000 vibrations per second (very high-pitched sounds). As people get older their ability to hear high-pitched sounds decreases. Other animals are able to hear sounds in different frequency ranges – dogs can hear higher-pitched sounds than humans can.

In music the note middle C is produced by a string vibrating at 256 vibrations per second. Doubling the frequency of the vibration to 512 vibrations per second produces a note one octave higher than middle C. Similarly, reducing the frequency to 128 vibrations per second produces a note one octave below middle C.

In a musical instrument the pitch of the sound can be changed in a variety of ways. In a wind instrument the pitch of the notes produced is changed by varying the length of the column of air in the instrument by covering more or fewer of the holes. In a guitar the pitch is varied by the thickness of the strings, the tension in the string or by the length of the string that is free to vibrate. For a percussion instrument the size of the instrument determines the frequency of the note produced. In a drum the pitch of the note can also be changed by increasing or decreasing the tension in the drum skin.

How we hear

When an object, for example a drum, is struck, sound waves will travel out in all directions. Some of these sound waves will reach the ear and travel down the ear canal to the eardrum. When the vibrations strike the eardrum it will start to vibrate. These vibrations are then passed through a series of bones in the inner ear and transmitted through a fluid-filled cavity called the cochlea. Here the vibrations activate nerve endings which transmit messages along a series of nerves to the brain.

In the brain this message is decoded and translated into the sound we 'hear'. As sound waves travel in straight lines it is easier to hear something if the head is turned so the ear is facing the sound. Animals such as dogs, horses and deer, which rely heavily on their sense of hearing, have ears which can swivel round to face in different directions. The more sound waves that reach the ear, the easier it is to hear quiet sounds. Some animals, such as foxes, rabbits and mice, have large ears so they can pick up sounds more easily.

Echoes

When sound waves hit a solid object such as a wall or a mountainside some of the sound will be absorbed but a large proportion will bounce off again. Sometimes this can create an echo and you will hear two versions of a sound – one that reaches the ear directly, and one that has travelled some distance, hit a solid object and then bounced back to your ear.

Children with hearing difficulties

Young children may have hearing impairments, either temporary or permanent, for a number of different reasons. Those children who are unable to 'hear' sounds need lots of opportunities to experience sound vibrations so they can build up an understanding of what different sounds 'feel' like.

Contexts for learning about sound

Babies

Exploring sound with babies is a good way to develop their **listening skills** and to encourage them to **use all their senses** to explore the world around them.

>> Find the sound

Wind up a musical toy or a small music box and hide it somewhere in the room. Draw attention to the music and ask the baby to help you find the music. Crawl alongside the baby to different places around the room. Don't go straight to the music box, but visit other places in the room first. Talk out loud while you are doing this:

- Where's the sound coming from?
- Is it here?
- No, it's not here, where can it be?

When you have found the source of the sound, celebrate together:

- Here it is, we've found it!

Repeat the game several times, hiding the music box in the same place and see if the baby goes straight to find it. Then try hiding it somewhere else, or try the same game outside and see how the baby reacts.

Observe:

- How the baby shows **curiosity** about the sound – in gesture, facial expression or posture.
- The speed with which the baby learns to **distinguish the sound** from other background noise.
- How quickly the baby begins to **predict** what will happen in the game.
- How **persistent** the baby is in trying to find the music box.

Bang the drum

Provide a range of everyday objects to use as drums. Empty tins of different sizes, metal and plastic bowls and aluminium foil pie dishes all work well. Plastic, wooden and metal spoons all make interesting beaters.

Comment as the baby plays the drums, talking about loud sounds and soft sounds.

Try playing some music, or singing a song with a strong rhythm while the baby is banging the drums.

Observe:

- The ways the baby **manipulates** the beaters and drums to create sounds.
- Any **preferences** which the baby demonstrates in their **choice** of drum or beater.
- **How long** the baby focuses on exploring the drums.
- How the baby **reacts** to the rhythm of the music.

Snapshot

Mia picks up a wooden egg shaker and waves it around. When she notices that it makes a noise she shakes it hard and holds it close to her friend Hari's ear. Hari looks round to see where the noise is coming from and gets a gentle tap on the head from Mia's enthusiastic shaking.

> Hari starts to cry and Mia drops the shaker and covers her ears to try and block out the noise.
>
> Mia and Hari are learning that that sound travels in all directions and that our ears are the organs which we hear with.

Toddlers

Encouraging children to listen carefully develops their **awareness of their senses** and how they use these to interpret what is happening in the world. Having to move quietly and concentrate on listening also builds **self-control** and develops **gross motor skills**.

≫ Find the timer

This is an exciting game to play which involves children in listening carefully and using their sense of hearing to solve a problem. Use a kitchen timer or alarm clock which makes a ticking noise. Without the children being able to see what you are doing, set the timer and then hide it somewhere in the room.

Explain to the children that you need to find the timer before it goes off and wakes everybody up. Encourage them to listen carefully and to try and track down the timer by the sound that it makes.

Vary the game by shortening the time, changing the place where the timer is hidden or by inviting one of the children to hide the timer.

Observe:

- How carefully the children **listen** to try and track down the sound.
- How well they **cooperate with one another** to try and find the timer.
- The degree of **self-control** they demonstrate in keeping quiet.
- How well they **concentrate** on the task and how **persistent** they are.

≫ What's that sound?

Take a small group of children outdoors and sit in a peaceful place. Ask the children to close their eyes and concentrate on listening to all the different sounds around them.

- What can you hear?
- Which sounds you recognize?
- Are there any sounds you don't know?
- How could we find out what they are?

Repeat this activity in the same place at different times of the day.

- Can you hear the same sounds?

Observe:

- How **confident** individual children are in closing their eyes and listening carefully.
- **How long** they can continue this activity.
- **The words they** use to describe the sounds they hear.
- The **ideas they have** about what might be making the sounds.

Snapshot

Jess gets out the basket of musical instruments and starts to investigate it. He drops one of the cymbals on the floor and delights in the response he gets when everybody turns to look at him. The practitioner models how to hold the cymbals and knock them against each other and Jess copies her. He gets up and marches around the room banging the cymbals and soon has a line of children following him.

Jess is learning about how sounds are made and how we use sounds to attract attention.

Preschool children

As young children practise **listening** to and making sounds in many different situations their ability to **distinguish between sounds** will increase. First-hand experience helps them to be more aware of the **volume and pitch** of different sounds and will enhance their ability to **compare, sort and classify sounds** effectively.

>> **Musical washing line**

This experience helps children to extend their understanding of the difference between the sounds that different material can make and encourages them to experiment with their own sound combinations.

What you need:

- A place to string up a washing line with objects hanging from it. This should be at a height where children can reach the objects to hit them.
- A selection of large and small kitchen tools made from different materials, for example, wooden spoons, metal ladles and plastic tongs, small pans, metal and plastic cups.

What to do:

- Look at the collection of kitchen tools with the children.
- Talk about what they are for and how you would use them.
- Discuss what sorts of materials the different tools are made of.
- Encourage the children to sort the tools into groups depending on what material the tools are made of.
- Introduce the idea of making a musical washing line.
- Ask the children to choose a selection of tools from each group that they think would work well on the musical washing line.
- Help the children to hang the tools on the line, evenly spaced.
- Choose a tool to use as a beater.
- Investigate the sounds which the tools make when they are hit with the beater.
- Investigate:

    o Which ones make a loud noise?
    o Which ones make a soft noise?
    o Which ones make a high sound?
    o Which make a low sound?
    o What happens when you use a beater made of a different material?

Observe:

- How the children **sort and classify** the materials.
- The **criteria they use** for choosing different objects.
- Any **predictions** they make about how the materials might sound.
- The **words they use** to describe the sounds they make.

Snapshot

Alex and Ben are playing outside. They pick up two sticks and use them to tap the side of the wooden shed. They create a banging noise which amuses them greatly. Their key person watches what they are doing and suggests they explore other places outside with their sticks to find out what sounds they can make. The boys find a metal bucket with a small volume of water in the bottom. When they hit the bucket it makes a loud ringing sound and the water in the bottom vibrates.

Alex and Ben are learning that different sounds are produced when wood and metal are struck and that the vibrations can make water move.

>> Speaking tube

This investigation helps children to focus on how different animals use their senses and on how humans can design tools to help them hear things more clearly.

What you need:

- A selection of books and pictures showing animals with large ears.
- A length of plastic tubing – hosepipe or fish pond tubing works well.
- Two large plastic funnels which will fit snugly into the ends of the tubing.

What to do:

Look at the pictures of animals with large ears and talk about how they use their ears to hear quiet sounds. Discuss the shape and size of the ears and the way in which the animal can move them.

Help the children to investigate what happens if you cup your hand behind your ear and then listen to a sound.

- Is it easier to hear soft sounds?

Investigate the tubing with the children. Try holding one end close to your ear and speak quietly into the other end.

Warn the children not to shout!

Push the funnels into either end of the tubing. Encourage one of the children to hold one of the funnels to his ear, and another child to speak quietly into the other funnel.

Help the children to experiment with talking and listening to each other through the speaking tube.

Observe:

- The **comments which the children make** about how different animals use their senses.
- How they **manipulate** the tubing and funnels to make the speaking tube.
- How they **cooperate with one another** to test the tube.
- The **ideas they suggest** about where to use the speaking tube.

Developing effective scientific communication

Having many different opportunities to explore sound, through making sounds, learning to listen carefully and developing the skills of distinguishing between sounds support not only children's scientific learning but also their language development. Hearing the 'vocabulary of sound' used by the practitioner in its correct scientific context will help children to develop and express their ideas and broaden their understanding.

sound	listen	ear	alarm
loud	speak	mouth	tick
soft	shout	music	noise
high	whisper	tune	drum
low	talk	tube	funnel

Open-ended questions which will encourage children to explore sounds could include:

- Can you find a way to make a very soft sound?
- How far away can you hear a radio playing?
- Which shaker makes the best sound?
- Could you play a tune on your musical washing line?
- Can you make a 'kitchen band'?

Equipment and resources

Children under 3

Simple musical instruments – hand bells, shakers, drum, maracas, wooden xylophone
Rainstick

Empty metal tins and large bowls
Wooden spoons and beaters
First Explorers Rainstick (*Reflections on Learning: www.reflectionsonlearning.co.uk*)
First Explorers Percussion frog (*Reflections on Learning: www.reflectionsonlearning. co.uk*)
CDs of music of different types

3 to 5 year olds

Musical instruments
Guiro percussion frog
Wind chimes
Rainstick
Short lengths of plastic tubing
Lengths of drainpipe
CDs of music of different types

Further reading

Harris, J. (2006) *Little Book of Sound Ideas.* Lutterworth: Featherstone Education.
Sherwood, E.A., Williams, R.A. and Rockwell, R.E. (1990) *More Mudpies and Magnets.* Beltsville, MD: Gryphon House.
Walker, R. (2005) *Dorling Kindersley Guide to the Human Body.* London: Dorling Kindersley.

12 | Light, Colour and Shadow

Chapter Summary

This chapter looks at the importance of light in our lives and at how we see things. It reviews the properties of transparent, translucent and opaque materials, answers the question about why the sky is blue and looks at the phenomenon of colour and how we appreciate it. How shadows are created is discussed and the way in which shadows change over the course of the day is explained.

Appreciating the potential of light, shadow and colour as resources to explore with young children provides an ever-changing resource for them to investigate. These are presented in the context of investigating light, exploring colours and developing children's understanding of how shadows are created.

Background knowledge

Light

Light and shadow are phenomena which are experienced every day, but are seldom given a great deal of attention. The presence or absence of natural light determines the rhythm of our daily life, influences the way homes and workplaces are designed and has a powerful effect on physical and psychological wellbeing.

Light is a form of radiation which is given out by a range of sources, including the sun, the stars, electric and fluorescent light bulbs, fire and candles. These are called primary light sources. The moon is not a primary source of light, it reflects the light of the sun. Similarly, shiny objects such as metal foil and mirrors are not primary sources of light; they only look bright because they reflect light. These are referred to as secondary light sources.

The sun is the most important source of light we experience and sunlight has a powerful effect on many aspects of our lives.

- The human body needs to have some exposure to sunlight in order to synthesize the essential vitamin, Vitamin D, which protects people from bone diseases such as rickets.
- However, prolonged exposure to strong sunlight can cause premature ageing of the skin and lead to cancer.
- Sunlight is an essential component of the process of photosynthesis by which plants grow and much of our food is produced.
- Sunlight can be used to provide energy through the use of solar panels and is also the original source of energy available to us through burning fossil fuels such as coal, oil and gas. These are all derived from plant materials laid down in the Earth's crust many billions of years ago.

How we 'see' things

Light from the sun, a light bulb or a candle travels outwards in straight lines, in all directions – we often talk about 'rays of light'. Some of these light rays enter the eye directly and we then 'see' the light source. When light falls on objects all around us, some is absorbed by the object while the rest bounces off from the surface. Light bouncing from the surface of an object enters the eye and we then 'see' that object.

The eye works in many ways like a camera. Light enters the eye through a hole at the front called the pupil. The pupil controls the amount of light which enters the eyeball. In bright light the pupil contracts to leave only a small hole for light to pass through. In poor light the pupil expands to allow as much light in as possible.

As the light enters the eye it passes through a transparent lens which bends the rays of light to focus them on the back of the eyeball. The back of the eyeball, the retina, is covered in nerve endings. These nerve endings are stimulated by light falling on them and transmit messages to the brain. In the brain the messages are translated into images which have shape, depth and colour – these are the objects we 'see'.

In some individuals the lens at the front of the eye may not be exactly the right shape to focus the rays of light on the back of the eyeball. In this case the person will be either short or long sighted and may have to use glasses or contact lenses in order to be able to see clearly.

Colour

Colour is all around us in the natural and man-made world; it is something which people react strongly to and which can affect their feelings of contentment and happiness.

The light which comes from the sun or from any other source of light is made up of a spectrum of electromagnetic energy of particular wavelengths which our eyes are sensitive to. These range from violet at the short wavelength end of the spectrum to red at the longer wavelength end. When light falls on an object some of the light waves are absorbed by the object and some are reflected. The wavelength of the reflected light which enters our eye determines the colour which we perceive the object to be. For example, if the reflected light is largely at the longer wavelength end of the spectrum the object will appear to us to be 'red', while if it is at the short wavelength end of the spectrum it will appear to be 'violet'.

We can see the different colours which make up the visible electromagnetic spectrum of light when we look at a rainbow. A rainbow forms when sunlight shines on drops of rain. As the light passes through the raindrop it is split up into a continuum of colour from red through to violet. The raindrops also act as tiny mirrors, reflecting the light back so we see a pattern of light which we call a rainbow. When Sir Isaac Newton identified the spectrum as being made up of the colours of the rainbow (red, orange, yellow, green, blue, indigo and violet) he described seven different colours because of his strong faith and the religious overtones of the number seven.

The colour of the spectrum – a rainbow effect – can also be seen on the surface of CDs, when the sun shines on an oily puddle of water and on the outside of a soap bubble just before it bursts. These effects are produced by the light rays of different wavelengths being reflected off the surfaces and back towards our eyes.

Why is the sky blue?

The answer to this intriguing question, lies in the way rays of light behave when they travel from the sun through the atmosphere to the surface of the Earth. Light from the sun is emitted at wavelengths right across the electromagnetic spectrum from short wavelength ultra violet light to longer wavelength infra red light.

As light passes through the atmosphere most of the longer wavelength red, orange and yellow light passes straight through but shorter wavelength blue light is absorbed by the gas particles in the atmosphere and then scattered in all directions. When you look up at the sky it is this scattered short wavelength light that you see as a blue sky.

Transparent, translucent and opaque

Some materials are defined by their ability to let light pass through them. A transparent material allows almost all of the light falling on it to pass through. If you look through a transparent material you will be able to see clearly the shape, outline and colour of objects on the other side of it.

Clear glass and clear plastic drink bottles are both examples of transparent materials.

A translucent material allows some light to pass through, but reflects or absorbs the rest. If you look through a translucent material you will be able to see the vague shape of an object behind it, but will not be able to make out the detail. Greaseproof paper and frosted glass are good examples of translucent materials.

A material which is opaque does not allow any light to pass through it – it either reflects or absorbs all of the light which falls on it. If a bright light is shone on an opaque material it will cast a shadow on the surface behind it.

Mirrors and reflective surfaces

When a beam of light strikes an object, light rays are scattered in all directions from the surface of the object. The rougher the surface the more random this scattering is. Conversely, if the surface is very smooth, such as a piece of metal, an acrylic mirror or a sheet of mirrored glass, the rays will tend to be reflected back in the direction they came. The smoother the surface, the brighter and clearer the reflected image will be.

A flat mirror, known as a plane mirror, gives a reflection that is the same size as the original and the same way up. Curved mirrors give different types of reflections because the light rays striking the mirror are reflected either inwards or outwards depending on the curve of the mirror. In a concave mirror – one that curves inwards – the light rays are reflected in towards one another and cross over at a point in front of the mirror. When you look in a concave mirror the reflection you see will be upside down because the reflected light rays have crossed over, transposing top and bottom, left and right. In a convex mirror – one facing outwards – the light rays are reflected away from one another so you are able to see a larger area of the surrounding room than you can in a plane mirror.

Shadows

A shadow is formed when a light shines on an opaque object, for example, a crayon. The light cannot pass through the crayon so behind it there will be a dark area where the light cannot reach – this is the crayon's shadow. Translucent objects such as pieces of frosted glass or some types of plastic can also create shadows. Because a translucent material allows some light to pass through, but absorbs or reflects the rest, the shadow that is formed will be lighter in colour.

The size and shape of a shadow depend on how close the light source is to the object, how bright the light is, how far away the object is from the surface that the shadow falls on and the angle at which the light falls on the object.

- If the light source is very close to the object the shadow will be large, if it is further away the shadow will be smaller.
- If the light source is bright, the shadow will have very distinct, sharp edges. The shadow will be only slightly larger than the object.
- If the object and the light source are moved away from the surface that the shadow falls on, the shadow will get bigger but the edges will become fuzzy and less distinct.
- Tilting the light source at an angle to the object changes the shape of the shadow, creating shadows that are long and thin or short and fat.

All these variables can be explored easily using a strong torch or an overhead projector – this is the best way to understand the different shadow effects which can be created.

Shadows out of doors

Shadows will appear to change in shape and position out of doors at different times of day. This is because of the rotation of the Earth around the sun. Early in the morning the sun will appear in the east and low in the sky. Shadows formed at this time will be very long and thin. As the Earth rotates on its axis the sun will appear to rise in the sky until at midday it is directly overhead. Shadows cast at this time of day will be very short and fat, and may hardly exist at all. During the afternoon the sun will then appear to sink in the sky towards the west. By late afternoon shadows will be long and thin again, but will also be pointing in the opposite direction from where they were in the morning.

Contexts for learning about light, shadow and colour

Babies

From a very young age babies are **curious** about their environment and should have opportunities to **explore** it **with all their senses**. This will increase their **confidence** and **independence**, and begin to build their early **understanding of colour** and the **differences between light and dark**.

⟫ Exploring light

Bring down the light levels in the room to give babies the sensation of darkness. To allay any fears be sure to create a peaceful, calm environment when you do this, perhaps by talking quietly to the children and playing soft music in the background.

Repeat this experience on several occasions, talking to the children about what they can see and what the dark 'feels' like.

Observe:

- How individual babies react to this experience – note their **facial expression, gestures,** and the **sounds** they may make.
- Which babies appear **confident** and which need to be reassured and comforted in this new environment.

Introduce a beam of light from a torch or a shaft of sunlight into the darkened environment.

Observe:

- How different babies react to the light – **the gestures, movements and sounds** they make.
- How **curious** they are about the light.
- How they try to **explore** it.
- The way they demonstrate that they are **asking questions** about how the light behaves.
- If the experience is repeated on several occasions, whether some babies begin to **make predictions** about how the light will behave.

⟫ Exploring shadows

When the sun shines look for the shadows which are created in your room at different times of day.

Place an interestingly shaped object on a sunny windowsill and draw the babies' attention to the shadow it creates.

Observe:

- How the babies demonstrate their **curiosity** about the shadow.
- Whether they reach out towards it. Whether they try to pick it up.
- If they **notice** that the shadow changes position during the day.
- If over the course of several days any of the babies begin to **predict** when and where the shadow will appear.

>> Exploring colour

Create some collections of coloured objects for babies to explore independently. Try a basket containing several examples of the same item in different colours or a range of different items that are all the same colour.

Observe:

- The way in which different babies **make choices** and **express preferences**.
- How they **handle** the objects.
- How some colours seem to be **preferred** over others.
- How long individual children **persist** with the activity.
- How babies **explore** a collection of objects that are all white.
- Whether they **explore** a collection of black objects in the same way.

Toddlers

Helping toddlers to change their environment by creating dark spaces, making shadow patterns and viewing the world from a different perspective builds on their **interest and curiosity**. They will be developing their powers of **observation** and building their **experience of materials** and how they behave.

>> Exploring light

Help the toddlers to create a dark den in a corner of the setting. This could be done by draping a thick blanket over a table, using a large cardboard box or utilising any small corner where the light levels can be turned down.

Provide small torches so the toddlers can explore the darkened space.

Observe:

- Which children are **confident** to **explore** the darkened space and which are more hesitant.
- How they **handle the torches** to find out about the space.
- The interactions that take place between different children. Whether girls are more **inquisitive** about the dark space than boys. Whether the children watch and **learn from one another**.
- What **questions** or comments they have about the experience.
- Whether they **select other resources** to take into the dark space **to find out** what they look like in the dark.

>> Exploring shadows

Set up an old-style* overhead projector on the floor, projecting onto a clear wall space. Encourage the toddlers to explore what happens when they put different objects on the surface of the projector.

Observe:

- The sorts of objects the children **choose** to put on the projector.
- How they move the shapes around to **create different effects**.
- **What they say** when they are playing with the overhead projector.
- How they interact and **communicate with one another**.
- How they **play and explore** the shadows which form on the wall.

(* 'Old-style' overhead projectors are safe to use with young children as the bulb is sealed in the base unit and the equipment is ventilated by a fan to keep it cool. DO NOT USE an overhead projector with the lamp in the top unit with young children, as these become very hot.)

>> Exploring colour

Provide a range of different coloured transparent materials for children to look through – coloured pieces of acetate, bottles of coloured water or coloured acrylic.

Observe:

- How the children **explore** the coloured transparent materials.
- How they **handle the materials**.

- What they **learn from one another**.
- What **comments** they make.
- **How long** they **persist** with their explorations.
- **How often** they return to the activity to repeat the experience.

Snapshot

Tyrone picks up a handful of coloured shapes and spreads them out on the light box. He moves the shapes around to create patterns and then lifts up a sheet of red acetate and looks at the shapes through this.

Tyrone is learning about the transparent, translucent and opaque properties of materials and about how different materials absorb or reflect light rays.

Preschool children

Building on their previous practical experience of light, shadow and colour, preschool children will be **posing questions, seeking explanations** and **developing their own theories** about how the world works. Adults can support this process by **providing interesting resources and challenges**, encouraging children to **observe** carefully and to **handle tools and materials confidently**.

≫ How many greens are there?

What you need:

- Collection of leaves from plants, shrubs and bushes around your setting.
- Shade cards or colour charts for paint.
- Coloured acetate sheets.
- Colour paddles.
- Light box or a bright, clean window.

What to do:

- Help the children to lay the leaves out on the surface of the light box. (Alternatively they could lay them out on a plain, light coloured surface next to a window).

- Look carefully together at each of the leaves. Ask the children to describe what they can see, and help them to notice the different shades of colour there are.
- How many different shades of green can you see?
- Can you think of names for all green colours?
- Try matching some of the leaf colours with the shades on the colour chart.
- Then encourage the children to look at the leaves through each of the coloured acetate sheets. Asks:
- What can you see now?
- Have the colours changed?

Encourage the children to go on investigating the leaves on the light box – discuss shape, size and texture as well as colour.

Observe:

- How they **sort and classify** the leaves.
- The **comments** that the children make about the leaves and the **ideas that they put forward**.
- Use these to prompt the **investigation** of other materials – **transparent, translucent and opaque**.

Take time at the end of this experience to talk with the children about what they have been doing. Listen carefully to their **ideas, observations, questions** and **comments**. These will suggest a number of new starting points for exploration.

   Snapshot

Jack and Malika are looking at a collection of shells. They feel the texture of the shells, knock them together to find out what they sound like and line them up in size order. The practitioner shows them the collection of paint shade cards and asks them if they can find any colours which exactly match the shells.

The children spend the next twenty minutes comparing the shades of colour on the paint cards to the colours they can see on the shells, talking all the time about how well the colours match.

Jack and Malika are learning about the characteristics of objects in the natural environment and are refining their skills in sorting and classifying.

≫ Shadow dance

What you need:

- A small group of children.
- A sunny day.
- An open area outside where the children will be able to see their shadows easily.

What to do:

Help the children to notice the shadows on the ground. Talk together about what shape they are, what size they are, what colour they appear to be.

Encourage the children to investigate all the different shadow shapes they can make with their bodies – by moving their arms around, sitting down, and standing up. Ask:

- What happens to your shadow?
- Who can make the tallest shadow?
- Who can make the smallest shadow?

Talk about where your shadow seems to join your body. Ask:

- What happens when you stand on one leg, hop or jump in the air?
- Can you make your shadow disappear?

Later in the day repeat this whole activity with the same group of children in the same place. Ask:

- What do you notice about the shadows now?

Observe:

- The **comments** that the children make about their shadows.
- How they **communicate their ideas** to one another.
- Any ways they think of to **measure** their shadows.
- What **connections** they make between their own bodies and the shape of their shadows.
- How they **explore** the best places to make shadows.
- What **association** they make between the position of the sun and the shadow that is created.
- Any **predictions** they make about how their shadows will behave.

Encourage the children to talk about their experiences with shadows. Listen to the ideas they volunteer and think about how you could provide opportunities for them to follow up on their ideas and take their investigations forward.

Developing effective scientific communication

When young children are exploring light, shadow and colour, adults will have many opportunities to introduce the correct scientific terminology into conversations and discussions. By modelling the use of these terms in everyday conversation you will be helping children to build their own range of vocabulary to describe what they see and experience.

sun	moon	star	sky
light	bright	sunlight	sunbeam
dark	shade	shadow	torch
eye	look	see	transparent
shape	size	tallest	smallest
colour	black	white	rainbow

Questions which pose challenges, encourage discussion or prompt further exploration or investigation will all help to develop young children's scientific thinking and investigative skills. Some possibilities are:

- Can you see in the dark?
- I wonder if you can make light go around corners?
- How long is your shadow?
- Does everything have a shadow?
- Which colour do you think it is easiest to see?
- How many different blues can you find?

Equipment and resources

Children under 3

Multi-purpose light box
Old-style overhead projector
Coloured acetate sheets
Acrylic splats
Colour paddles
Large acrylic shapes
Mirror Exploratory
Large acrylic mirrors
Baby kaleidoscope mirror
Triptych mirror
Wall mirrors
Horizontal mirrors
(All from Reflections on Learning: www.reflectionsonlearning.co.uk)

Large torch
Shiny aluminium containers and foil

3 to 5 year olds

Light boxes and light panels
Old-style overhead projector
Coloured acetate sheet
Fraction circles and squares
Attribute shapes
Square transparent counters
Round transparent counters
Translucent coloured tangram shapes
Mirror exploratory
Large kaleidoscope mirror
Triptych mirror
Table top triptych
Message mirrors
Wall mirrors
(*All from Reflections on Learning: www.reflectionsonlearning.co.uk*)
Torches
Aluminium foil
Collections of transparent, translucent and opaque materials
Shadow puppets

Further reading

Brunton, P. and Thornton, L. (2004) *The Little Book of Light and Shadow*. Lutterworth: Featherstone Education.
Ferri, G. (ed.) (1990) *Everything Has a Shadow, Except Ants*. Reggio Emilia, Italy: Reggio Children.
Williams, R.A., Rockwell, R.E. and Sherwood, E.A. (1987) *Mudpies to Magnets*. Beltsville, MD: Gryphon House.

13   The Earth

Chapter Summary

In this chapter the structure of the Earth and its place in the solar system are explored. There is information on the Earth in relation to the sun and the planets, the moon and the influence it has on the tides and an explanation of why we experience night and day and the changing seasons. The origins of different types of weather are looked at and the structure of the rocks which make up the Earth is described.

This creates the context for providing young children with experiences which will help them to build their awareness of the structure of the natural environment we live in and of the influence which weather has on our daily lives.

Background information

The Earth in space

The passage of time through day and night and the changing seasons of the year have a fundamental impact on our lives. They determine the way we organize our daily lives, the homes we build, the clothes we wear and the journeys we take for business or pleasure. From a very early age children will be aware of the difference between night and day and of the influence which the weather has on what they are able to do each day. They will also be aware of the sun, the moon and the stars and may well be curious about what they are and why they are there.

The solar system

The Earth is one of the eight planets in our solar system, orbiting around the sun. In order of distance from the sun these planets are: Mercury, Venus, Earth, Mars, Jupiter, Saturn, Uranus, and Neptune. Pluto, which used to be regarded as the ninth planet in the solar system, is now defined as a dwarf planet.

The International Astronomical Union (IAU) defines a planet as 'an object in orbit around the Sun that is large enough (massive enough) to have its self-gravity pull itself into a round (or nearly round) shape. In addition a planet orbits in a clear path around the Sun – there are no other bodies in its path that it must sweep up as it goes around the Sun'.

The sun is a star which emits light and heat energy. It appears large to us on Earth because it is closer than the other stars in the galaxy. The stars are in the sky all through the day and night; we can only see the stars at night because of the brightness of the sun during the day. The planets are secondary sources of light as they reflect the light of the sun. This is why we can sometimes see planets such as Venus in the sky at night.

The sun is a huge body and comprises more than 99% of the total mass of the solar system. It therefore exerts a strong gravitational pull which keeps the planets in orbit around it (see Chapter 7). The time it takes for the Earth to orbit once around the sun is 365.25 days. This is equivalent to one Earth year, with the 0.25 days being accumulated to give us an extra day in February every fourth year – a leap year. The other planets orbit the sun at different rates so a year on Mercury lasts only 88 Earth days and a year on Mars lasts 687 Earth days.

The Moon

The moon is a large body which orbits the Earth. Like the planets, the moon is a secondary source of light, reflecting the light of the sun. The moon is held in its orbit by the gravitational pull exerted on it by the Earth (see Chapter 7). Other planets also have moons – Mars has two and Jupiter has at least sixteen.

The moon orbits around the Earth every 28 days (one lunar month) and as it does so it appears to change shape depending where it is in its orbit. The shape of the moon stays the same; it just looks different depending on what proportion of it is illuminated by the sun at any given time. At the beginning of a lunar month the new moon is barely visible at all, but by 14 days later the whole surface is visible as a full moon. When the moon is full it can be very bright, bright enough to cast pale shadows of opaque objects.

Tides

Water makes up approximately 70 per cent of the surface of the Earth. Tides are caused by the gravitational pull of the moon on this large body of water causing sea levels to rise and fall twice a day. The pull of the moon is strongest when the moon, the sun and the Earth are in line with one another during their orbits. This occurs at the time of the new moon and, a fortnight later, at full moon. This gives rise to a spring tide – a very high tide followed by a very low tide. The gravitational pull of the moon is at its least when it is in the first and last quarter of its orbit. This gives rise to neap tides, where there is a much smaller gap between the heights of high and low tide.

Night and day

As the Earth is orbiting around the sun it is also rotating on its axis, one revolution taking 24 hours. This means that one side of the Earth is facing towards the sun and the other side is facing away from the sun. As the Earth rotates an observer standing at any point on its surface will gain the impression that the sun is moving across the sky. As we are all aware it is the Earth which is moving, not the sun. The Earth rotates on its axis in an anti-clockwise direction so the sun appears to rise in east and set in the west.

Seasons

The change in seasons throughout the year – the variations in temperature and the length of daylight – is caused by the fact that the Earth is tilted on its axis relative to the sun. This means that in winter the northern hemisphere is tilted away from the sun so the temperature is lower and the days are shorter. Conversely, in summer the northern hemisphere is tilted towards the sun so the temperature is higher and the days are longer.

In summer in the UK we experience approximately 18 hours of daylight, the longest day being the 21st June. On the shortest day – 21st December – there are only approximately eight hours of daylight. Between these two dates – on 21st March and 21st September – are the spring and autumn equinoxes when we experience 12 hours of daylight and 12 hours of darkness.

At the two Poles the effect of the Earth's tilt is at its most extreme, resulting in 24 hours of darkness in winter and 24 hours of daylight in summer. At the Equator the tilt of the Earth has no effect, so days and nights are 12 hours long right throughout the year.

Weather

The changes in light and temperature which occur as the seasons change have an impact on the circulation of air through the atmosphere. As a general rule air movement occurs from areas of high pressure to areas of low pressure and from the warmer Equator to the colder Poles. When the sun warms the air in a specific location the air rises, creating an area of low pressure. More air then rushes in from the surrounding areas to fill the space, creating wind. As well as the sun influencing the circulation of air around the world, ocean currents such as the Gulf Stream and local weather patterns also have an influence.

Rain, hail and snow

Rainfall occurs when the water vapour in the air in the clouds condenses into liquid water forming droplets that are heavy enough to fall to the ground. The movement of water from the sea through evaporation into the atmosphere and then back to the ground again as rain is known as the water cycle (see Chapter 8).

Hailstones are formed in thunderclouds when ice crystals are moved around within the cloud building up layer after layer of ice as they do so. Eventually the hailstones become too heavy to stay up in the cloud and they fall to the ground as hail.

Snow is formed when tiny ice crystals in the clouds stick to one another and form crystalline patterns known as snowflakes. The temperature at which this happens determines the size and shape of the snowflakes, ranging from small dry powdery snow at very low temperatures to large wet flakes at higher temperatures. Every snowflake has its own unique pattern.

Humidity, dew and frost

All air contains water in its gaseous state, known as water vapour. This water comes from the soil and from the surrounding plants and trees. The relative amount of water vapour in the air is known as humidity – in tropical rain forests humidity is very high and in deserts humidity is very low.

Warm air can hold more water vapour than cold air. As the temperature falls at night the air close to the ground cools down and water vapour condenses back into water. This is what we recognize as dew.

If the temperature of the air at ground level falls below 0° C the water vapour in the air freezes and forms frost. Frost can cause a great deal of damage, to plants, to water pipes, and to rocks and stones. Frost damages plants because the liquid inside the cells of the plant turns into ice which then damages the structure of the cell and the affected part of the plant dies. Frost bursts water pipes because water expands as it freezes into ice, and can exert enough pressure on the pipe to fracture it. Frost damage to rocks is part of the weathering process described in more detail below.

Structure of the Earth

The Earth is made up of a central core surrounded by layers of molten rock called magma and covered by a crust of rock on the surface. The rocks which make up the Earth's crust fall into three categories – igneous, sedimentary and metamorphic rocks – depending on how they were formed.

Igneous rocks are formed when magma rises towards the surface and cools down to form solid rock. If the magma cools slowly the rock-forming minerals it contains crystallize out slowly to form large crystals. Granite is a good example of this. If the magma spills out from the surface in a volcanic eruption the rock will cool very quickly and only very tiny crystals will form. Pumice and volcanic ash are examples of this type of igneous rock.

Sedimentary rocks are formed when the rocks of the Earth's crust are broken down by the process of weathering and are carried away to a different location by rivers, glaciers or the sea. These fragments of rock mix with the other particulate material, such as sand, silt, shells and plant material in the sediment and settle in thick layers. Over time the layers are gradually compressed as more and more layers of sediment are laid down on top.

The structure and properties of sedimentary rocks are determined by the nature of the original material they are derived from. For example, sand turns into sandstone, silt turns into shale, calcium shells turn into limestone, silica shells into flint and plant materials into peat, coal or bitumen.

Fossils are found in sedimentary rocks when dead animals or plants become trapped in a layer of mud or sand. As more layers pile up on top the sand or mud becomes squashed and turns into rock. The plant or animal skeleton then rots away and the space becomes filled with other rocks and minerals, preserving the exact outline of the original animal or plant. The quicker the sediment forms the more likely it is that a specimen will be preserved as a fossil, so the largest number of fossils can be found in sedimentary rocks such as chalk.

Fossil fuels – coal, gas and oil – are created through the deposition of plant material or plankton which becomes compacted and subjected to very high temperature and pressure. Over a very long period of time this material changes in chemical composition to form the fuel sources we currently rely on.

The third category of rocks, metamorphic rocks, is formed when igneous, sedimentary or metamorphic rocks are changed through the action of heat or pressure. This occurs in those parts of the Earth's crust which are most unstable – in areas where volcanoes or earthquakes are common and where rocks grind together to produce excessive pressure. Heat converts igneous rocks into gneiss or schist and limestone into marble. Pressure can convert shale into slate.

Recognising rocks

Rocks can be distinguished by their colour, structure, hardness and by the uses we put them to. For example:

- Chalk is made of soft limestone and is used for mark making.
- Slate splits into flat plates and is used for tiles and roofing.
- Marble is made of hard limestone and is used to decorate buildings and to create sculptures.
- Granite is a hard igneous rock used for building.
- Sand is mixed with gravel and cement to make concrete.

Weathering of rocks

Over time rocks break down into smaller pieces through the action of weathering. This is a very slow process, occurring over millions of years, but nevertheless it has resulted in the shape of the Earth's crust as we recognize it today. Rocks can be weathered by the action of rain, wind, ice, mechanical pressure or chemical action.

For example, the sun shining on the surface of a large rock will heat it up and cause it to expand slightly. At night when the temperature falls and the rock contracts again. Over time this will cause small cracks to form which will fill up with water when it rains. If the temperature falls below 0° the water will then freeze and expand into ice, eventually cracking the rock. Pieces of rock will break away and many will be carried along in rivers where they will knock against one another and break down further. Eventually these small pieces of rock will be deposited as soil.

Sand and clay

Sand is formed from the weathering of rocks into small particles and varies in colour depending on the composition of the rock it is derived from. The sand on white tropical beaches is derived from the breakdown of limestone, shells and coral, while the black sand found on some of the beaches of Tenerife is made up of tiny particles of volcanic basalt. Sand which contains a large amount of iron will be a deep yellow colour. Sand made up of large particles can feel very coarse and abrasive, but sand composed of very small particles feels very cool and soft. Because sand is made up of small particles it can be poured like a liquid (see Chapter 6).

Clay is also a particulate material but in this instance the particles are suspended in water. It varies in colour and composition depending on the exact nature of the minerals it is derived from. Adding water to solid clay transforms it into a soft slippery material which can be cut, rolled and flattened. When it has dried out it can be made workable again by adding water, but once it has been heated it undergoes a chemical change into a hard waterproof material and this change cannot be reversed (see Chapter 6).

Contexts for learning about the Earth

Babies

First-hand experience of the natural world helps babies to connect with their environment and to **enjoy the experience** of being outdoors in all weathers. This establishes firm foundations on which to build **positive attitudes** to playing and exploring outdoors as children get older and start to **make choices** for themselves.

≫ Experiencing weather

Introduce babies to the many different types of weather we have in the United Kingdom by taking them outdoors, whatever the weather.

Before going out draw the babies' attention to the weather by looking out of the window and talking about what you can see.

Talk about whether it will be warm or cold outside, sunny or raining, breezy or still.

As you are dressing the babies to go outside talk about the different articles of clothing they are putting on and whether these will keep them dry or warm or cool.

Once outside, draw the babies' attention to the weather they are experiencing by talking about what you can see and how it feels. For example:

- On rainy days explore the rain dripping off leaves and branches and look for places where the soil has become muddy and puddles have formed.
- On sunny days draw attention to how warm it feels and look at the shadows made by the trees and by yourselves.
- On windy days help the babies to experience the sensation of wind in their faces and look for streamers and flags blowing in the breeze.
- On very cold days explore frost and ice and, if you are very lucky, snow.

Observe:

- How **interested** and **curious** the babies are about the experiences they are having.
- How they **use their senses** to **explore** the world around them.
- How **confident** they are about new experiences.

≫ Exploring pebbles

Make a collection of large smooth pebbles for the babies to explore. Include a wide a range of colours as possible including some pebbles that are too large for them to lift up. Make sure none of the pebbles are so small that they could create a choking hazard.

Encourage the babies to explore the pebbles – what they feel like, what they sound like, how easy they are to lift up, whether they feel cool or warm.

Observe:

- How they handle and **manipulate** the pebbles.
- Which of their **senses** they use to find out about the pebbles.
- **What they try to do** with them.
- **How long** individual babies play with the pebbles.

Snapshot

Molly and her key person are outside on a windy day. As the wind blows in her face Molly closes her eyes, puffs her cheeks out and blows out.

Molly is discovering the power of the wind and is thinking creatively as she makes connections between different experiences.

Toddlers

Exploring natural resources like sand builds children's **early understanding of different materials**, where they come from and how they behave. There are opportunities to **plan how things should be done** and find **practical**

solutions to problems. Exploring in the dark engages children's **curiosity**, builds their **self-confidence** and provides an opportunity to talk about **feelings and emotions**.

How can we empty the sandpit?

This is an activity for the outdoor sand area where there is plenty of space for moving sand around on a grand scale.

Explain to the children that you would like their help to empty out the sandpit.

Provide them with a range of buckets of different sizes along with spades, scoops and trowels and a tarpaulin or groundsheet and let them get to work.

While they are digging talk to them about what the sand feels like, how easy it is to scoop it up and how heavy it is to lift.

As they empty the sand out help them to notice the conical shape that it makes when it is poured.

Encourage the children to cooperate so they can move heavier loads of sand together.

Add some water to the sand in the sandpit. Investigate what this does to the sand. Ask them:

- How has it changed?
- Is it easier to dig up?
- What shapes does the sand make now when it is poured?

Observe:

- **How interested** different children are in the challenge which has been posed.
- **How long** they persist in the task.
- How they **handle** the tools.
- The **comments they make** to describe the sand and how it behaves.
- How they **cooperate** with one another.

Out in the dark

In winter, as it gets dark quite early, it is often possible to explore the outdoor area using torches. It is important to know your children well so you can gauge who will find this experience exciting and who might be intimidated by it. Share your planning for this activity with the children's parents so they can reinforce the safety messages you will want to convey to the children.

Build up to this experience over several days by looking out of the window and drawing children's attention to the darkness outside.

Explore how well torches can help us to see in the dark by encouraging the children to explore some darker places indoors. For example, under a table or in a room with the lights turned down.

Once everyone is prepared for the experience, give a small group of children a torch each and take them outside to explore. Talk to them about what they can see and about their feelings about being outside after dark.

Observe:

- How **confident** individual children are.
- How they **handle** the torches.
- How they demonstrate their **feelings and emotions**.
- The way they describe what they can see.

Preschool children

Observing and talking about the weather will give children the opportunity to **notice and talk about features of their natural environment** and to think about different ways to **record information**. They will be using their **skills of observation** to look in more detail at natural materials and applying different ways of **sorting and classifying** natural materials.

>> **Exploring the weather**

What you need:

- A selection of flags, streamers, windmills, balloons.
- Wind chimes.
- Plastic beakers for collecting rainwater.
- A selection of stories about the weather. This could include:

    The Wind Blew by Pat Hutchins
    Alfie Weather by Shirley Hughes
    After the Storm by Nick Butterworth
    Maisy's Wonderful Weather Book by Lucy Cousins
    The Sunny Day by Anita Milbourne

What to do:

Talk to the children about the different types of weather we experience in the UK.

Read some of the weather stories together and talk about the weather outside that day. Ask:

• What do you think it will feel like outside today?
• What sort of clothes should we wear when we go out?

Set up some weather-recording equipment out of doors. Streamers, flags or balloons tied to a fence or a post can be used to record how windy it is. A plastic beaker placed in a shallow hole in an open spot will serve as a rain collector. Ask:

• Which way are the streamers blowing today?
• How breezy is it?
• Are the streamers/balloons hanging down limply or are they being blown out straight?
• How strong does the wind feel?
• Is it strong enough to blow you along?
• Is it windy enough to make the wind chimes tinkle?
• Is it raining outside?
• Will we have to put our coats and boots on?
• How much water have we collected in our rain catcher?

Talk about different ways of remembering what the weather is like each day. This could include taking photographs or recording the daily weather on a chart. Discuss the sort of symbols you might use to record the weather – children may well be familiar with the symbols which are used on TV weather forecasts.

Choose a time each day to check on the weather and record it on your chart. Ask:

• What should we use to record a rainy day – a raindrop? An umbrella? A rain hat?
• What would a sunny day look like on our chart?
• Can we use our chart to find out how many sunny days we had last week?

Observe:

• How the children **recall** their experiences of the weather when you are reading the stories together.
• **The ideas** they suggest for suitable clothing for different types of weather.
• The words they use to **describe** the types of weather they experience.

- How they **collect and record the information** that they gather about the weather.
- How they **interpret that information** on the chart or in the photographs when they describe the weekly weather pattern.

⟫ Rock detectives

What you need:

- A selection of colour paint cards from a DIY store.
- A collection of stones, rocks and pebbles.
- Magnifying glasses.
- A stand magnifier.

What to do:

Encourage the children to look closely at the collection of stones and pebbles. Ask:

- What do they feel like?
- Can you find any sharp spiky stones?
- Are any of the stones smooth?

Look carefully with the magnifying glass or the stand magnifier. Ask:

- What can you see?
- Can you see shapes or patterns in the stones?
- Are all the stones the same colour?
- Can you sort them into different colours?
- Are some of the stones more than one colour?

Allow the children to choose their favourite stone. Ask:

- Can you tell me what it looks like?
- Can you match the colours in your stone to the colours on the paint card?
- Do they match exactly?
- Do you need more than one colour chart?

Encourage each child to choose one of the paint cards and to take it outside to see if they can find anything which exactly matches the colours on his/her chart. Ask:

- What did you find?
- Can you describe the colours to me?

Observe:

- How **observant** individual children are.
- How they **express their ideas** about what their stones look like.
- **How much time** they spend **comparing** the stones and the colour charts.
- The different ways in which they **sort and classify** the stones.

Developing effective scientific communication

In order to describe natural phenomena accurately young children need a wide range of scientific language to draw on. Exploring alongside the children, and talking out load about what interests and puzzles you or about what you have discovered, will help them to see how particular terminology can be used in different situations. Language you might introduce includes:

weather	rain	sun	wind
breeze	fog	frost	snow
flag	streamer	windmill	balloon
blow	gust	storm	cloud
rock	stone	shape	heavy
light	sharp	smooth	colour
same	different	match	chart

Asking questions and posing problems can extend and deepen young children's thinking and will create a context for many other productive investigations. Possible challenges could include:

- Finding out if all sand looks and feels the same.
- Investigating what happens when water is added to dried clay.
- Investigating which is better for building – dry sand or wet sand.
- Exploring how many different ways there are to sort a rock collection.
- Investigating what happens when water is tipped down a slope of sand.

Equipment and resources

Children under 3

Large wooden hand lens
Sheet magnifiers

Large stand magnifier
Large plastic 'discovery' trays
Child-sized trowels and spades
Sandpit tools
Transparent plastic buckets
Clear plastic beakers and jugs
Windmills and steamers
Wind chimes
Woven wicker baskets
Sisal baskets
Collections of large pebbles and stones

3 to 5 year olds

Large and small magnifiers
Large stand magnifier
Sheet magnifiers
Small acrylic mirrors
Collectors' trays
Large plastic 'discovery' trays
Child-sized trowels and spades
Sandpit tools
Sieves
Plastic beakers and jugs
Collections of rocks and stones in attractive containers
Paint shade cards
Fossils
Mineral samples
Windmills and streamers
Wind chimes
Weather chart
Weather symbols

Further reading

Brunton, P. and Thornton, L. (2006) *Little Book of Treasureboxes*. Lutterworth: Featherstone Education.

De Boo, M. (ed.) (2005) *Early Years Handbook*. Hatfield: Association for Science Education.

Young, T. and Elliott, S. (2003) *Just Discover! Connecting young children with the natural world*. Victoria, Aus: Tertiary Press.

References

Association for Science Education (ASE) (2001) *Be Safe!* (3rd edition). Hatfield: ASE.

Bertram, T. and Pascal, C. (2002) 'What counts in early learning', in O.N. Saracho and B. Spodek (eds), *Contemporary Perspectives in Early Childhood Curriculum.* Greenwich, CT: Information Age. pp. 241–56.

Brunton, P. and Thornton, L. (2006) *Exploring Together: Inspiring family learning.* Londan: Featherstone Education.

Ceppi, G. and Zini, M. (eds) (1998) *Children, Spaces, Relations: Metaproject for an environment for young children.* Reggio Emilia: Reggio Children.

Community Playthings (2002) *Spaces.* New York: Community Products.

Community Playthings (2008) *I Made a Unicorn.* Robertsbridge: Community Products UK.

Council for the Curriculum, Examinations and Assessment (CCEA) (1997) *Curricular Guidance for Pre-School Education.* Belfast: CCEA. Available at http://www.deni.gov.uk/preschool_curricular-2.pdfth

Council for the Curriculum, Examinations and Assessment (CCEA) (2006) *Understanding the Foundation Stage.* Belfast: CCEA. Available at www.nicurriculum. org.uk/foundation_stage/index.asp

Curtis, D. and Carter, M. (2003) *Designs for Living and Learning.* St. Paul, MN: Redleaf.

Davis, D. and Howe, A. (2003) *Teaching Science and Design Technology in the Early Years.* London: David Fulton.

Department for Children, Education, Lifelong Learning and Skills (DCELLS) (2008) *Foundation Phase: Framework for children's learning for 3 to 7 year olds in Wales.* Cardiff: Welsh Assembly Government.

Department for Children, Schools and Families (DCSF) (2007) *Confident, Capable and Creative: Supporting boys' achievements* (000682-2007BKT-EN). London: DCSF.

Department for Education and Skills (DfES) (2007) *The Early Years Foundation Stage* (00012-20007PCK-EN). London: DfES.

Farrow, S. (1999) *The Really Useful Science Book.* London: Falmer.

Filer, J. (2008) *Healthy, Active and Outside.* London: David Fulton.

Giudici, C., Rinaldi, C. and Krechevsky, M. (eds) (2001) *Making Learning Visible: Children as group and individual learners.* Reggio Emilia: Reggio Children.

Goldsworthy, A. and Feasey, R. (1997) *Making Sense of Primary Science Investigations.* London: ASE.

Gopnick, A., Meltzoff, A.N. and Kuhl, P.K. (1999) *The Scientist in the Crib.* New York: William Morrow.

Greenman, J. (1988) *Caring Spaces, Learning Places: Children's environments that work.* Redmond, WA: Exchange.

Harlen, W. (2000) *The Teaching of Science in Primary Schools* (3rd edition). London: David Fulton.

Harlen, W. (2001) *Primary Science: Taking the Plunge* (2nd edition). London: Heinneman.

Hughes, A.M. (2006) *Developing Play for the Under 3s*. London: David Fulton.

International Astronomical Union (IAU) (n.d.) website at http://www.iau.org/public_press/news/release/iau0603/questions_answers/

Isaacs, B. (2006) *Bringing the Montessori Approach to Your Early Years Practice*. London: David Fulton.

Johnstone, J. (2005) *Early Explorations in Science* (2nd edition). Maidenhead: Open University.

Jordan, B. (2009) 'Scaffolding learning and co-constructing understandings', in A. Anning, J. Cullen and M. Fleer (eds), *Early Childhood Education Society and Culture* (2nd edition). London: SAGE.

Katz, L.G. (1993) *Dispositions: Definitions and implications for early childhood practices.* (Catalog No 211, ERIC/EECE: Monograph series no. 4). Available at http://ceep.crc.uiuc.edu/eecearchive/books/disposit.html

Katz, L.G. (2009) *Developing Children's Innate Dispositions.* Available at http://childrensmuseumblog.blogspot.com/2009/01/developing-childrens-innate.html

Learning and Teaching Scotland (2006) *Birth to Three.* Available at http://www.ltscotland.org.uk/earlyyears/about/birthtothree/guidance.asp

Learning and Teaching Scotland (2009) *Curriculum for Excellence.* Available at http://www.ltscotland.org.uk/curriculumforexcellence/publications/Buildingthecurriculum2/index.asp

Lindon, J. (1999) *Too Safe for their Own Good*. London: NCB.

Malaguzzi, L. (1998) 'History, ideas and basic philosophy', in C.P. Edwards, L. Gandini and G. Forman (eds), *The Hundred Languages of Children: The Reggio Emilia approach – advanced reflections* (2nd edition). Stamford, CT: Ablex. pp. 49–97.

Nicol, J. (2006) *Bringing the Steiner Waldorf Approach to your Early Years Practice*. London: David Fulton.

Ouvry, M. (2000) *Exercising Muscles and Minds*. London: NCB.

Peacock, G.A. (1998) *Science for Primary Teachers*. London: Letts Educational.

Piazza, G. (1999) *UK Study Tour*. Reggio Emilia: Reggio Children.

Rinaldi, C. (1997) 'A mother cat and her kittens', in T. Filippini and V. Vecchi (eds), *The Hundred Languages of Children: Narrative of the Possible*. Reggio Emilia: Reggio Children. p. 182.

Robson, S. (2006) *Developing Thinking and Understanding in Young Children*. London: Routledge.

Smith, B. (2004) *The Science You Need to Know*. Hatfield: ASE.

Thornton, L. and Brunton, P. (2009) *Understanding the Reggio Approach* (2nd edition). London: David Fulton.

White, J. (2008) *Playing and Learning Outdoors*. London: Routledge.

Index